The Christmas I'll Never Forget

David C. Reyes

The Christmas I'll Never Forget

CrossLink Publishing
www.crosslinkpublishing.com

ISBN 978-1-936746-27-9

Unless otherwise indicated, all scripture quotations are taken from the Holy Bible, King James Version, Cambridge, 1769.

Preface

This story takes me back to a very special time in my life. Perhaps obscured for many years in the recesses of my mind, I drew upon these memories when the idea came about to write this book. Growing up on a small ranch myself, I learned the phase; "to work by the sweat of your brow." My father instilled a work ethic in me at an early age, as he used to say; "hard work brings about its own reward." However, while I was busy tending to my chores, working by the sweat of my brow showed little reward at the time. Waking up at the crack of dawn to clean, candle, and box the chicken eggs, was a laborious task. To add to my thoughts of the senselessness of it all, my father sold those eggs for a fraction of what "farm fresh eggs" would normally sell for. My father, who was a route delivery driver, would take the eggs into work with him and sell them to the other drivers. Apparently his joy came from simply providing a "home-grown product," not making a profit.

Besides tending to the chickens, we had a goat, a couple of steers, and two horses. And even though I was thoroughly excited to receive a horse on my birthday, it wasn't too long before that excitement soon faded. Besides all the other chores associated with having animals, work with the horses required long, sometimes tedious, hours. Washing, brushing of hair, mane and tail, was fun and exciting in the beginning; but after a couple of years, it soon lacked its luster.

Of course being a young teen there were many other activities going on in my life at the time. Entering my high school years, there were after-school sports, church activities, and of course girls—the latter taking up more of my mental time, than physical. Yet when I arrived at home it was back to my chores, cleaning out the chicken coops and raking out the manure from the horse corrals. When my father came home from work, he would often come help me with any unfinished chores, or maybe we would make a run to the feed store. During that time, we would talk about current events, or other subjects which were taking place in my life at the time.

As time went on, events would transpire in our lives, where we no longer had the ranch. However years later at family gatherings, I would find myself articulating those events with fond memories. I guess what I didn't realize, was I should have enjoyed the journey of that special time in my life, instead of always asking, "What was in it for me." From the laborious hours of building those corrals, to setting up countless fencing posts . . . each hammer and nail was forging an irreplaceable bond between father and son.

Looking back, my father and I threw the football around like most father and son do. Yet my fondest memories were the hours spent, "working by the sweat of my brow." And although I never realized it at the time; my father was right. Hard work brings about its own reward. I just never realized that forging those lasting memories was a part of that reward...

Table of Contents

Chapter One ~ Stable Hand

The coolness of the morning awoke Luke Dawson as he gathered his patchwork quilt made by his grandmother and snuggled beneath its covers. The comfort of its weight reminded Luke of the many times when "Nana" would come over to the house bearing her homemade blueberry pancake mix in an old ceramic pitcher to make them breakfast. The aroma of bacon sizzling in the kitchen and the morning chatter with his parents; were now but memories since her and grandpa's passing. Now the ranch next to theirs was occupied by the Wheeler family and was one of only a handful of homes within site of the Dawson cabin. Living in northeastern Washington State near the Rocky Mountain foothills, they would soon be bracing for another cold winter.

I'll sure be glad when this week is over and we can be on Christmas vacation.

As Luke pondered those thoughts, the family rooster crowed out a reminder it was time to get up. The morning routine so familiar since his childhood brought back fond memories. The images passed through his mind of he and his brother Ben playing pirates in the loft of their barn - boasting twig branches as their swords. However those times were now distant memories with the coming of his brother's illness. Stretching out the sleep from his body, he glanced at the clock once more.

5:45..., I guess I better think about getting up before Mattie or Ben hogs up the bathroom.

Reluctantly uncovering himself and placing his feet in a pair of worn out slippers, much too small for his growing twelve year old feet; he grabbed his robe and headed for the bathroom. Mattie, his younger sister of six, greeted him in the hallway.

"♫...Good morning, good morning, good morning, to you...♫" as she sang a cheerful melody from the Kellogg's Corn Flakes commercial.

"You're in an awfully good mood this morning," hugging her with a soft kiss on her rosy cheeks.

"I am…! Today we start to make Christmas cards at school. Mrs. McCarthy said we get to work on them each day this week. Luke…, do you think I should make two cards for both mommy and daddy, or just one for the two of them?"

Luke drew a thought from the corner of his eye. "I think since this is going to be your Christmas present to them, you should make one for each of them. Besides…, Mom will want hers to be more girly and stuff, and Dad's should be manlier."

"Okay, I will. Luke…"

"Yes…"

"How come Ben is always sick and just lies around all the time?"

"They don't know Mattie. Mom and Dad have taken him to a lot of doctors, but no one seems to know what's wrong with him."

Her soft blue eyes filled with concern. "Is he going to be alright? Isn't there some medicine they can give him?"

"Like I said, they don't know what's wrong with him or why he is always tired and has no energy. Or why he gets faint sometimes and is always throwing up. One doctor thought he might have what they call Anorexia, but then they're not sure because he tries to eat plenty of food. They say if you have Anorexia, that you don't want to eat anything so they're not sure. I just hope the doctors find out soon, because for being fourteen years old, he is way too thin and he seems to be getting worse."

Hearing their voices, their mother Sandi Dawson, called out from the kitchen.

"Ben, Luke, Mattie…, get washed up and ready for breakfast! Time is wasting and you're going to miss the bus for school. Luke…, have you fed the animals this morning?"

"No, not yet Mom, I'll get to it right after breakfast."

Feeding the ranch animals was a routine Luke knew very well. As As far back as he could remember he and his brother were up at the crack of dawn tending to the livestock. In some ways, sharing that time with his brother was a labor of love. But recently with all the chores falling on him - it was just labor.

As the Dawson family gathered at the kitchen table, Mr. Harold Dawson told everyone to hold hands to say grace.

"Father in heaven, we thank you for the many blessing of our lives. We pray for those this morning that perhaps don't have food on their tables like we are blessed to have. I thank you for my family sitting at this table, and I pray for your hand upon them during this day, amen."

"Amen," the rest of the family followed.

The family dug-in to scrambled eggs and country potatoes. Mrs. Dawson noticed her son Benjamin reluctantly staring at his breakfast. She placed a caring hand upon his shoulder.

"Benny, aren't you hungry this morning?"

"I don't know, I thought I was doing alright, but then right now I had diarrhea. I hope I'm not going to have one of those days. It's so embarrassing to have to keep asking my teachers to be excused from class to go to the bathroom."

"Your teachers don't give you a hard time about it, do they?"

"No not at all. They all understand I have this condition, so they are all pretty good about it."

Mattie noticed the downcast look on her brother's face. She turned to him, as her warm smile beamed with hope.

"Benny..., did you write to Santa Claus to tell him what you want for Christmas this year? I already sent my letter to Santa Claus asking him to bring me a Barbie Dream House. But if you want, I can write another letter so he can bring you something too."

Knowing the reality of the whole Santa Claus situation, he thought to choose his words carefully.

"Mattie, that's so nice of you to want to ask Santa Claus to bring me something. But right now I would just settle on not feeling sick all the time. That's all I could hope for this Christmas."

"Amen to that," Mr. Dawson added. "Amen to that."

Luke finished getting dressed for school, and grabbed his plaid winter coat hanging on a coatrack near the front door. With the winter season upon them, the temperatures were getting down near freezing overnight. As he headed out to the barn to feed the animals, his father grabbed his coat as well and followed after him.

"Son…, hold-on there a second. I want to talk to you about something."

"Sure Dad, but I need to start feeding these chickens while we talk, otherwise I will be late for school."

Taking hold of an old Folgers coffee can, he dug deep into a large bag of feed mash to give to the chickens. Making his way along the line of chicken cages he filled the tray, and made sure the drip water system was at the proper level. His father began to separate a couple of leafs of alfalfa to help him out, and threw them into a feeding trough in the corral to give to the steers. Luke turned his attention toward his father.

"So Dad…, what did you want to talk to me about?"

"Well son…, it's about this coming Christmas and fact that we are not doing very well financially right now. With the housing market being slow in construction, I'm not getting as many hours as I used to. Also, with all your brother's medical expenses, it's starting to put us in the hole. Bob Harper of Harper's Feed & Stables told me the other day he is looking for some temporary help in taking care of his horses and other duties. I know you and your brother have always loved horses, but since we can't afford to buy one, at least you could be around them if you took that job. I'm sure besides feeding and cleaning their pens, Bob will let you ride them once in a while. If you agree to work for him, you would start once Christmas vacation begins. I told him that on Sunday's you would have to do the work in the afternoons because of church in the mornings."

Mr. Dawson walked over and placed a caring hand on his shoulder. Luke sensing his father's serious disposition stopped what he was doing to face him.

"Luke…, I really need you to do this son. Ben can barely manage going to school, let alone work a physical job. If we are going to have any kind of Christmas this year, it will be from you making that extra income. As you heard at breakfast, your sister is so looking forward to 'Santa Claus' bringing her that doll house. I would also like to get something for your mother, and of course for you and Ben. Luke…, your brother is not doing well and the doctors still have not figured out what's wrong with him. Son, we're hoping it's not…, but this could be Ben's last Christmas."

The words pierced his heart like a double-edge sword. A deep concern grew on his face.

"What…? No Dad, not Benny!"

"I'm afraid so son. He seems to be going down-hill fast and the doctors have said that if he continues to get weaker and loses more weight, he might only have six months left."

"No Dad, he can't die, Benny's too young; he's just fourteen years old!"

"I know son, I can't bear the thought of that either."

Luke walked over to the corral and opened the faucet to fill a large aluminum water basin for the steers to drink. As the water flowed from the faucet, so did his tears for his brother. After gathering himself and wiping his tears on his coat sleeve, he came back into the barn to gather the eggs which had been laid overnight. Now thinking about their earlier conversation, he questioned his father.

"Dad, I'm only twelve…, can I work for Mr. Harper at my age?"

"Yes, the work you will be doing falls under the work exemption of agricultural or farming work. As long as you work during vacation time and not during regular school days, you can work a job. However, next year in 1978, some new laws are going to change to where you can only work during summer vacation."

"Okay Dad, I'll do it. I understand about Benny, and of course Mattie is too young. But it's just seems unfair that I'm the one who gets stuck with all the work around here."

"I know you do, and sometimes it seems that life is unfair and maybe it is. But I have learned that even though we don't understand why things happen at different times in our lives, there is usually a reason for it. Perhaps someday you'll understand why you were the one that gets stuck with all the chores around here. Who knows, maybe one of these days you're going to be a famous bodybuilder like that man Arnold Schwarzenegger. Perhaps this is your training to build big muscles," his father said while playfully tousling his chestnut brown hair.

"Funny Dad," as Luke rolled his eyes at his father's teasing.

"Anyway son, I appreciate you doing this for the family. And don't mention this to your sister about how serious Ben's condition is. You know how sensitive Mattie is, and if she knew things were as serious as they are, she would be crying all the time. I want all of us to enjoy a nice Christmas this year. And I especially want it to be so special for Ben…, a Christmas he'll never forget."

Luke promptly finished his chores, then grabbed his sack lunch from the kitchen table and headed out the door. Ben and Mattie joined him and they made their way to the main road to catch the bus. Being from a small town like Timber Falls, the elementary and middle-school which Luke and Mattie attended was all at the same location. Ben's high school was about a half-mile up the road. As the bus pulled into the high school parking lot, Luke watched his brother gingerly exit the bus and slowly make his way towards the entrance of the school. As Ben turned to wave goodbye, it brought to mind what his father had told him earlier about his condition. As Luke waved goodbye in return, he swallowed the lump in his throat from the thought that he could soon be watching his brother enter the school for the last time.

Luke and Mattie arrived at their school and separated with a warm hug. Carrie Wheeler from the ranch next to theirs began to walk with him to class.

"Hi Luke…, how are you doing this morning?"

He exhaled a labored breath. "Oh, you know, so-so."

"Is something wrong?" as she placed her hand on his shoulder to let him know her sincere concern.

"Nothing, I'm just worried about Ben, that's all."

"How is he doing?"

A pensive stare drew upon his face. "Not too good. He just seems to be getting worse."

"I'm sorry to hear that. Isn't there anything the doctors can do for him?"

"Carrie…, thanks for asking about him, but I don't feel like talking about it right now; if that's alright."

"Okay, I understand. I'll be saying a special prayer for him."

"Thank you Carrie, he certainly needs all of our prayers."

The school day came to a close. Luke and Mattie entered the bus which proceeded over to the high school. As the high school students began to board, they noticed that Ben was not one of those entering the bus.

"Luke…, Ben didn't get on the bus. Do you think mommy had to come pick him up because he got sick again?"

"Probably... That's like the third time in the last couple of weeks he has gotten too sick to finish the day."

Luke ran a caring hand down her shoulder length hair. "Mattie…, can you please pray for Benny? More than ever he needs our prayers."

Seeing the emotions stem from him, she placed her soft little hand on top of his.

"Don't worry, Luke, he'll be alright, I just know it."

Seeing his sister's firm resolve, he questioned her response. "Mattie…, why did you say that you know Ben will be alright?"

A sense of hope filled her smile. "Because of the song we sing in children's church."

"What song is that?"

"You know that one…, the one that says he's able. It goes like this..."

♫… He's able, he's able, I know he's able…, I know my God is able to carry me through. He healed the broken hearted, he set the captives free…, he healed the sick and he raised the dead, and he caused the blind to see… He's able, he's able, I know he's able…, I know my God is able to carry me through …♫

"So you see Luke, it says that God is able to heal the sick. That's how come I know he can heal Benny and make him feel all better."

As Luke saw this childlike faith stem from his little sister, it warmed his heart. But what he didn't want to tell her is although miracles sometimes happen, they don't happen that often. He just hoped that her childlike faith would not be shattered if his brother's condition did not improve.

As they continued on their way home in his rural community, Luke signaled the driver of his wishes to exit at the next stop.

"Mattie…, I need to get off here and see Mr. Harper about working for him. Make sure you go straight home when you get off the bus. I don't want you going around looking for butterflies or running around like you do sometimes - just go straight home."

"Butterflies...? Butterflies don't come out in the winter; they come out in the spring, silly. And don't worry, I'll go straight home."

"Okay good. Remind Mom that I went to see Mr. Harper today about that job."

"I will."

Luke exited the bus and made his way down Double-A Ranch Road over to where Harper's Feed & Stables was located. Harper's Feed & Stables was the sole feed store in the area, which also provided boarding of horses. It had been an iconic symbol of stability in the town ever since Luke could remember. Upon arriving at the storefront entrance, Luke stood patiently, as Mr. Harper finished up his business with a customer. When he was finished, he acknowledged him with a firm handshake.

"Well hello there, Luke. Your father told me you would be by to see about helping me with some temporary work."

"Yes sir, that's why I'm here. I would like that job if I could."

"Well, let me take a look at you son," as he eyed him up and down and grabbed a hold of his bicep muscle. "Hum..., you seem pretty strong for your age. You're twelve years old, right?"

"Yes sir, thirteen in April. I do all the chores around our house, like feeding our animals and cleaning out their pens."

"Well first of all..., call me Bob. And secondly..., the job is yours if you can lift one of those fifty-pound sacks of grain over there."

Luke promptly picked-up one of the sacks, and flung it over his shoulder with ease.

"How's that Mr. Harper?"

"Very good Luke, the job is yours. You can go ahead and set the sack of grain back down. Now the minimum wage in this state is $2.75 an hour, but I'm going to pay you $3.00 an hour. Part of the reason why I need help right now is that my son is going on vacation, and so he can't help me during the holidays. Now..., did your father tell you this job is only for the next couple of weeks?"

"Yes sir, I know. But our family needs some extra money for Christmas this year."

"Well since you are here, I'll show you around a bit. Why don't you go out back and I'll meet up with you in a minute. I need to lock up the cash register."

"Okay, I'll head on out back."

Mr. Harper began to button things up in the storefront, as Luke wandered around back and walked into the horse stable. Beginning with the first horse, he began to greet each one by their names that were posted on a placard outside of each horse stall.

"Hello there Lightning… I imagine by your name that you are a fast runner. And seeing how you are a Thoroughbred, you must be very fast." He walked over to the next stall. "Next to Lightning…, we have Mama's Corn Bread. I understand why they call you that, seeing how you are a light bay almost like the color of cornbread. And next…, we have Spotty's Castle. And since you are an Appaloosa with spots on your hind-end, your name fits you. Now on the other side of the stable, we have Captain Morgan. I think your name is pretty obvious considering you are a sturdy Morgan horse. Then next to Captain Morgan…, we have Dusty. I'm not exactly sure about your name, but maybe they call you Dusty because you have a light dusting of white near the bottom of each of your hooves. And last…, we have Sundance."

Luke peered into the last stall to greet the last one. The horse turned its head and right away came up and nuzzled its nose against him.

"Wow, you're a friendly boy…; or are you a girl?"

Luke bent down to see what gender the horse was, when a voice startled him from behind.

"Sundance is a filly. She's just about three years old."

"Oh hi Mr. Harper. I was just getting acquainted with all your horses here."

"Well, most of them are not mine. Only Dusty and Sundance are mine, all the rest are boarded."

The two stood discussing the different breeds of the horses, when Sundance once again nuzzled its nose against him.

"She must really like you, Luke. It's not like Sundance to take to people. She usually keeps her distance and doesn't allow anyone to get too close to her."

"Mr. Harper…, I think I figured out why most of the horses are named what they are; but why is she called Sundance?"

"Well, the story of Sundance is kind of long, and I have a truckload of hay that just showed up. We can talk about Sundance some more while I unload the bales of hay."

Luke began to help unload the flatbed trailer of hay, while they continued with their conversation.

"Well Luke, the story of Sundance starts with her mother. Her mother's name was Reyna, which in Spanish means queen. And let me tell you, she was definitely a queen. She was a beautiful Quarter Horse with a silky-brown coat and great lines. When she ran through the fields, she stood-out above all the rest. As you might have noticed, we have over fifty acres in the back property where we let the horses roam free during the spring and summer months. Well, one year Reyna got pregnant and in the springtime she had a little foal. During the morning as the sun's rays would shine upon this little foal's back, she would get up and start to walk around in circles — first to the left, and then to the right. As she was doing that, she would bob her head up and down, and would start bucking all over the place. It was really a site to see as this little foal seemed to be dancing. Well, when my wife and I saw her do that, we decided to call her Sundance, because she liked to dance in the morning sun. When Sundance was just about a yearling, her mother got a terrible case of colic and we didn't catch it on time. Unfortunately little Sundance was by her mother's side when she died. After that, Sundance seemed to go into a kind of depression, and from that day on…, she never danced in the morning sun again. Well, anyway, that's the story of Sundance."

"Can she be ridden, is she broken in?"

"Yes, you can ride her. In fact part of your job will be to get those horses out and about for some exercise. Like I said, during the spring and summer months we let them run free in the back acreage; but now that it's winter, we keep them in their stalls."

"That's good, I really like to ride. My brother Ben used to enjoy riding too, but he has kind of lost interest in horses. I still want one, but we can't afford to buy one."

"Well, during the next couple of weeks you are going to get plenty of riding in."

Luke scanned the horse stable, storefront and horse corrals. "So Mr. Harper…, what else are my job duties?"

"Well, besides feeding the horses and cleaning out their stalls, you will make sure they are all cleaned and brushed down. Also, as you can see when a delivery comes in, you will come and help me with unloading the shipment. Then at the end of the day, take at least one of the horses out for a ride in the back trails to get some exercise. Your father told me you took riding lessons so I assume you know how to ride well. There is some stocking of merchandise and a few other chores here and there, but basically that's it. If you have any questions, just come and ask me. If for some reason I'm not here, just knock on the main house and my wife can help you."

"Okay, is there something else you want me to do this afternoon?"

"No, my son isn't leaving until next Friday, so you can officially start on that following Saturday morning. I just wanted to go over your job duties while you were here."

"Okay, I'll see you first thing next Saturday morning."

"Very good Luke, I'll see you then."

Arriving at home that evening, Luke hung his coat and blew on his hands from the chill in the air.

"Boy it's getting cold out. Do you want me to start a fire, Mom?"

"No, not right now, we're just about ready to have dinner. Get washed up and tell your brother and sister that dinner will be ready in about five minutes."

Luke gave a courtesy knock on the door, and entered his room which he shared with his brother. Taking off his shirt, his brother looked down at his feet with an inquisitive stare.

"What's that all over your shoes?"

Looking down, he saw some greenish mesh stuck to the bottom and sides of his shoe.

"Oh man, I should have taken my shoes off at the front door…; that's horse pucky."

"Horse pucky…? Why do you have horse pucky on your shoes?"

"I went to see Mr. Harper about that job. He was showing me around the horse stables, and I guess I got some on my shoes while I was in there."

"Oh yeah, I heard you are going to be working at Harper's over Christmas vacation. Is there a particular reason why you wanted to get a job?"

Luke recalled the conversation with his father. Knowing that some of the money he was going to earn was going towards a gift for him, he thought better of telling him the reason why.

"I just wanted to Benny. I can earn a little extra money and I get to be around horses. There's this one horse named Sundance that has already taken a liking to me. It will be so much fun to ride her and all the other horses."

Ben attempted to answer back, but began to gag and quickly ran to the bathroom. After a few minutes, Luke went down the hall and lightly knocked on the door.

"You okay, Benny?"

"Yeah, I'll be out in a minute."

Luke returned to his room and finished changing his clothes, to get ready for dinner. A few minutes later, Ben returned and lay on his bed.

"Luke, tell mom I'm not going to eat tonight. I think I'll just have a 7-Up and some saltine crackers here in my room."

"Are you sure? Mom made your favorite; fried chicken with biscuits and gravy."

"I know, and it smells good, but my stomach is upset right now."

"Alright, I'll tell her that you're not feeling well."

Luke began to leave the room to go to dinner, when Ben called out to him.

"Luke…"

"Yeah…"

"I just wanted to tell you that you're a good brother. I know we never say that kind of stuff to each other, but I just wanted you to know that."

"Thanks, you're a good brother too," as he questioned in his mind why his brother had said it the way he did.

As they sat around the dinner table, Mr. Dawson asked Luke about his day.

"So..., did you get everything straightened out with Bob Harper?"

"Yes sir. I went right after school and he showed me around the stables. He also told me what I will be doing as far as my job duties. He's going to pay me $3.00 an hour. That's a little more than minimum wage."

"Very good. Will you be working a full eight-hour day?"

"No, for six hours. I'll work from eight in the morning until three o'clock in the afternoon, with a one-hour lunch break. If I work those six hours for the full two weeks, I will earn a little over two hundred dollars."

"Very good, son. But don't forget, you still have your chores around here."

"Yes sir. I know I still have my own chores as well."

Mattie, eating only the skin off her fried chicken, turned her attention towards her mother.

"Guess what mommy...; I'm making some Christmas presents for our family in school."

"You are?"

"Yes, I'm making one for you and daddy, and one for Ben and one for Luke."

"Very good sweetie, we are so looking forward to your presents."

Drawing a thought, a look of concern grew upon her face. "Mommy, daddy..., have I been a good girl this year? I can't remember if I was good all year long, and I want Santa Claus to bring me my Barbie Dream House."

Mr. Dawson turned to his wife with a warm smile; as his little daughter's question melted his heart.

"Yes honey, you have been a very good girl this year. And perhaps this year, Santa Claus may be able to bring you that doll house. But if for some reason he can't, he will get you something else that you need. It's kind of in the same way that God works. God will give us what we need in our lives, and not necessarily what we ask for."

"I know I can't always get the toys I want, but I'm hoping this year I will. I might get what I want, because I was a good girl this year, right daddy?"

"Yes honey, you were a very good girl."

Taking a sip of her milk, she gathered another thought. "Oh, I almost forgot another thing... In our Sunday school class we are going to be doing a Christmas play, and I am going to be in it!"

"You are?" her mother questioned.

"Yes, we're doing a different kind of play."

"What do you mean by, a different kind of play?"

"I don't know, Sister Anderson said the play is not a tra..., transitional play or something like that."

"Oh, she probably meant it's not going to be a traditional Christmas play."

"Yes, that's what she said."

"Well then, that should be very interesting to see. Are you going to perform the play for the Christmas Eve service?"

"Yes, and she asked us if one of our older brothers could be in it too; so I told her that Luke would be in it."

Luke sat up straighter in his seat. He immediately turned to his sister with slight irritation.

"Me...? Why did you tell her that I would do it?"

"Because there's a part in the play where a boy has to be bigger than us; like a bully. So when Sister Anderson asked us, I thought of you because you are a big strong boy."

"So you volunteered me without asking me first, Mattie?"

"I didn't volumteer you. I just told Sister Anderson that you would do it."

"Mattie, you're saying it wrong. It's not volumteered, it's volunteered, with an 'n'."

"Okay, I didn't know."

"Mattie, you shouldn't have done that, because I don't know if I have time to be in that play. They are probably going to want to practice a lot and I'm going to be working for Mr. Harper during Christmas vacation. You shouldn't have done that Mattie."

Hearing his scolding tone, Mattie hung her head low as the tears began to form in her sparkling blue eyes.

"Mattie what's wrong, why are you about to cry?" her mother asked with concern.

"Because I did something wrong…! I did that volunteer thing and now Luke is mad at me! That means that I'm not a good girl anymore and Santa Claus won't bring me my doll house!"

She got up from the kitchen table, and rushed to her room in tears. Mrs. Dawson started to go after her, when Luke got out of his seat.

"No Mom, let me go talk to her. I didn't mean to get her upset, but she went and volunteered me without asking me first."

"I know and it's not your fault. But you know how sensitive she is, especially right now when she's counting on getting that doll house."

Luke entered Mattie's room to see her crying face down on her bed. He sat down next to her, and placed his hand caringly on top of her shoulder. Immediately she turned and hugged him tight.

"I'm sorry Luke…! I'm sorry I did a bad thing!"

"No Mattie, it's alright, don't cry," as he held her close. "You're not a bad girl, you're a good girl. In fact, you're a very good girl."

"I am?" as she sniffled and wiped a tear with the back of her little hand.

"Mattie, you made a mistake that's all, but that doesn't make you a bad girl. Look…, just because you make one mistake, that doesn't make you a bad person. God looks at us as a whole. He looks at all the different things you do throughout the year. Just because you make one mistake, he's not going to punish you for it. In the same way, Santa Claus isn't going to look at one mistake and not bring you something for Christmas. Mattie, you're just six years old; you're supposed to make mistakes. The thing that Mom and Dad always tell me is to learn from your mistakes, so you don't make them again."

Hope filled her eyes. "So you think I'll still get my doll house?"

"Yes, I can almost guarantee it."

"Luke, what does guarantee mean?"

"It means I am almost sure you will get your doll house."

"Really…?"

"Yes."

Her tear-filled eyes turned to joy, as she hugged him tight.

"Thank you Luke! You're the bestest brother! Well..., both you and Benny."

"I'm the bestest, huh? Well I think we need to work on your vocabulary their sis. Now let's go back into the kitchen and finish eating dinner, okay?"

"Okay..., and thank you for telling me that I'm a good girl."

"You are Mattie, so don't you worry about it, okay?"

"Okay..."

Chapter Two ~ By the Sweat of my Brow

The week passed quickly, and on the final day of school heading into Christmas vacation, Luke exited his last class and hurried to his locker. Placing his books inside, he walked over to where the elementary school kids were letting out. He quickly found Mattie and hurried her along as she said goodbye to a few classmates.

"Come on Mattie let's get going; moms waiting for us."

"Why is mommy coming to pick us up?"

"I told you this morning. I asked her to pick us up so she can drop me off at Harper's. I want to get in a few extra hours working at the feed and stables. I called Mr. Harper on Wednesday, and he said I could work for a few hours this afternoon."

She shuffled her feet to try to catch up. "Well I'm trying to hurry up, but my legs are littler than yours."

He stopped and took a hold of her backpack. "Alright, then let me carry this for you, that way you can walk faster."

"Okay, but be careful. I have the Christmas cards I made for you in there."

He placed her backpack over his shoulder. "Don't worry; I'll be careful with it."

As they waited at the curbside, Mrs. Dawson pulled up and they piled into the car. Ben was already sitting in the front seat, as Mrs. Dawson had picked him up first. Luke leaned forward in his seat.

"Hey Benny, how are you doing?"

"Alright, it was one of my better days."

"That's good. You do seem to have better color in your face today."

"Yes, and I'm glad that it's Christmas vacation. That way I can get some rest and not have to concentrate of my school work."

"Well speaking of work..., I start my job over at Harpers this afternoon."

"Yeah I heard. I wish I could work myself, but with my condition and all, it's too hard for me."

"Don't worry about it. Just get your rest and I'll tend to the work." Gathering a thought, he tapped his mother on the shoulder. "Hey Mom…, wasn't that one of the things that was a result of Adam and Eve's sin?"

"What's that, Luke?"

"That we men would have to work by the sweat of our brow."

"Yes, that's true. And we women would have to endure pain when our babies are born."

Upon hearing their conversation, an inquisitive look rose on Mattie face.

"Mommy…, why is there pain when a woman has babies?"

With a look of concern, she thought of how to answer her young daughter.

"Well sweetie…, we will talk about that when you're a little older. But all you need to know is the pain a woman goes through is well worth it, the second she holds that newborn baby in her arms."

Confusion drew upon Mattie's face. "But I still don't understand why there is pain when the stork brings you the baby. Does the stork bite you when you try to take the baby from it?"

Glancing at one another, Luke and Ben tried to hold their laughter.

Mrs. Dawson answered vaguely. "Like I told you before sweetie, when the time is right I'll explain it to you."

"Okay…, but I have another question... Why isn't there a stork in the pictures of the manger scene with the baby Jesus? There are cows, sheep and goats in the manger, but you don't see the stork. Shouldn't the stork be in the picture since the stork delivered the baby?"

"Well sweetie, I think Mary had a little bit of involvement in delivering that baby, but let's not talk about that anymore. So how was your day? Did you get finished with the Christmas presents you were working on?"

"Yes, I got them all done. I hope you like them, but some of the glitter fell off of yours and Benny's."

"That's okay, if it came from your heart, then I am sure we are going to love them."

Arriving at Harpers Feed and Stables, Luke exited the car.

"Mom..., I'm going to work until around six o'clock this afternoon. Since it's already getting dark at that time, Mr. Harper said that he or his wife would bring me home."

"Okay, but just be careful and do a good job for Bob. We have known their family for years and I don't want to hear that you did not do a good job for him."

"Don't worry, I will. Like I said...; I'll be doing this work, by the sweat of my brow."

When Luke arrived at the storefront, he saw that Mr. Harper was busy with a customer buying a sack of dry dog food. After the man chit-chatted with Mr. Harper about the local news in Timber Falls, he turned to pick up the sack. Seeing an opportunity to assist, Luke promptly took a hold of the sack and flung it over his shoulder.

"I'll get that for you sir."

"Well thank you, young man. You can place it in the back of my pickup truck."

Luke carried the sack to his truck, as the man turned his attention back to Mr. Harper.

"So Bob..., I see you got yourself a fine helper."

"Yes, Luke is Harold's son..., Harold Dawson."

"No..., not little Lukie... Why I remember the Dawson boys when they were no bigger than a couple of grasshoppers."

"Yes, Luke is helping me over the Christmas Holiday. Jeffrey is going on vacation with some of his friends, so Luke is filling in. You know how it is; teens his age want to spend the holidays with their friends instead of family."

As Luke was busy checking things out in the storeroom, Bob whispered to the man whose name was Ronald Friedman.

"Ron..., you mentioned you remember the Dawson boys. Well I don't know if you have heard..., but the brother Ben, is in a bad way."

"A bad way..., how is that?"

"He's got some kind of illness and the boy is going downhill fast."

"Really...? I assume he has seen Doctor Jenkins about his condition."

"Yes, and they have sent him to a specialist in Spokane, but they can't seem to figure out what's wrong with him. They were pin-pointing it to that new illness that is becoming more well-known called Anorexia."

"Does the boy not want to eat?"

"Well that's just the thing. The boy wants to eat, but he throws it up and he seems to be getting thinner and weaker all the time."

"Hmm..., well hopefully the specialist in Spokane can figure out what he has."

"Yes I hope so. Now is that all you need Ron? Do you don't need any grain or hay?"

"No, I am getting too old to be tending after livestock anymore. The wife and I have two labs and that's all we can handle in our lives right now."

Mr. Harper glanced at the clock on the wall. "Well it's been good talking to you Ron. However I better get going; I have more work to do this afternoon."

"Alright Bob, I'll be talking to you another time."

About that time, Luke returned to the storefront. Bob walked him Over to the stables and unlocked the door to the storage room.

"Luke..., this is where all the supplies are kept for the horses. We have a barrel of grain, a sweet-feed mixture, salt blocks, and all the riding equipment is stored in this room. Don't give them too much sweet-feed, just maybe once a week. If you give them too much, the males get all worked up wanting to get to the females when they're in heat. We also keep this storage area closed and locked at all times. There are a lot of critters in the area that come around looking for something to eat. Especially the raccoons who have figured out how to open the door latch. So after you are done, you need to make sure you lock the door."

"Yes sir, I will. We have raccoon problems at home also. They are always trying to get to the chickens and their eggs. However, what we did is we extended our fence so the dog can patrol that area. Our dog Misty is half wolf and half Alaskan Husky. She is so nice and sweet with people, but don't let her near other animals or she'll try to tear them apart. The raccoons stay clear of our chicken coops because of her."

Mr. Harper closed the storage room door, and proceeded with his instructions.

"Well Luke, your duties for today, is to feed the horses and then transfer the bags of grain on the side of the barn to the storefront. As you probably saw, there is a list of prices on the chalkboard. Just adjust the label maker to the prices written on the board and label each one. Since you will only be working a few hours today, that's all you have to do this afternoon. After you are done with that, I'll see about taking you home."

Luke got right to work placing a bag of grain in a wheelbarrow to feed the horses. As he began with the first horse next to the storage room, his thoughts went to his brother and his failing condition.

Oh Lord, please help Benny. Benny doesn't deserve to die. Why is it that bad things happen to good people? It just seems that life is so unfair at times. Why can't the Hitler's or the Charles Manson's of the world be punished by sickness, why Benny. That is something I never understood in life. Please God..., receiving presents and all that is fine to get, but what we need this Christmas..., is a miracle.

He began to feed each horse, moving from one stall to the next. Then he came upon the last one, which was Sundance. As he started to give her some feed, he continued to talk to the Lord in an audible voice.

"And just like this horse right here, Lord. Why did her mother have to die when she wasn't even a year old? Like Mr. Harper said, it caused her so much pain that now she doesn't dance in the morning sun anymore. That's no way to live your life being sad for the loss of a loved one. I'm sure Sundance loved her mother, so why did she have to die? And look at us; what if Benny dies and then what? Our whole family is going to be so sad that I can't even imagine it. And what about poor little Mattie; she is going to cry and cry for days. I remember when Mattie was about three years old and she would sit on Benny's lap and he would read her all kinds of stories. As he was reading, she would look at him in amazement that these lines of letters could create a story so interesting and full of life. But if Benny dies, then the life will be gone from those pages..., he will be gone. Mattie is too little to understand and will probably be like Sundance here. She isn't going to understand why someone she loved was taken away from her. Please God..., if you are listening to me ramble on like this, please do something..., you can't let Benny die!"

Luke continued raking out the stall, when Sundance playfully nudged him with her nose. He affectionately returned the gesture with a firm pat on her neck.

"Hey there Sundance... I know you probably didn't understand what I was saying right now, but I was just talking about you. I was thinking about how awful it must have been when your mother died when you were just a young filly. I have a brother and he isn't doing very well right now; and I just prayed that he doesn't die. Maybe you can understand how I feel. I haven't lost my brother yet, but if something were to happen to him, maybe I wouldn't want to dance anymore either. Not that I dance, but maybe I wouldn't want to do what I like to do, and that's writing. You see, no one knows about this, but I like to write stories. I keep a book of these stories hidden in my closet at home. I keep it hidden, because I don't want anyone to know, especially my dad. My dad is a tough man and if he knew I like to write stories, he might think it was sissy. In fact, you're the first person or animal I have told this to. But you know, somehow, someway..., I think you understand me. Or maybe you can understand the tone of my voice. Well that's what my dad tells me that animals can pick up on the tone we use to understand what we're telling them. Sometime this week we will go for a ride, okay? Maybe a nice ride is what we both need. For you to get out of this stall and get some exercise. And for me..., maybe it will keep my mind off of Benny - at least for a little while."

*****

The next morning, Luke was up at the crack of dawn and walked into the kitchen. He noticed his mother staring out the window; as the image of the family barn was just beginning to take form in the darkness of the passing night.

"Hey, Mom..."

"Morning, Luke..."

"What were you doing just staring out the window?"

"Just thinking…" as she cusped the coffee cup in her hands to gather its warmth.

"Thinking of what?"

"Oh, I just thinking how my mother used to come over and have a cup of coffee with me in the mornings. I remember how she used to point out all the little things she thought I was doing wrong in raising you kids. Sometimes I would get so upset with her for doing that, but she was my mother, so what could I do. Now sitting here, I miss her so much and wish she was still here. Maybe she would be able to tell me what I'm doing wrong, and why things are the way they are."

Opening the kitchen cabinet, he took down a box of cereal.

"Mom, you're not doing anything wrong in raising us. I think you do a great job."

"I don't know about that; just look at your brother. I must not be a good mother to allow this to happen to Ben," as the emotions stemmed from her voice.

"It's not anything you have done; you're not to blame for Benny being sick."

"Thank you for saying that, but I feel so helpless."

"I feel that way too. In fact I was just thinking about that yesterday when I was at Harpers working with the horses. I just don't understand why bad things happen to good people, or why like in Benny's case…, he has to go through this pain and suffering."

She took a sip of her coffee. "Son, I know the good book tells us that there is a reason for everything happening and that God has everything in control. But in times like these, it's so hard to keep the faith."

"I know, believe me, I know."

He began to pour the cereal into a bowl, when his mother stopped him.

"Wait Luke, we're out of milk, I'll have to pick some up today. What I think I'll do is take you to your job at Harpers and then I'll drive through the dairy to get some more milk. Do you want me to make you a bowl of oatmeal? I can use some pet milk instead of the regular milk."

"Yeah, I guess that would be alright, I'll make some toast to go along with it."

"Okay, let me fix you that oatmeal, and then we can get on our way."

After breakfast, Mrs. Dawson drove Luke out to Harper's making it there just as the eight o'clock hour began. Mr. Harper gave a quick wave to Mrs. Dawson, as Luke greeted him with a slight shiver.

"It's awfully chilly out, isn't it Mr. Harper?"

"Good morning Luke..., yes it is a little chilly. They say we might be looking at a good snow in about a week, maybe in time for Christmas."

"I hope so; a good snow would be really nice. Usually we have way more snow by this time of year."

"Yes, that's true. But what did I tell you about calling me Mr. Harper; you can call me Bob."

"I know, but my father always taught me to respect our elders and to call grown-ups sir or ma'am, or mister and misses; I'm just used to it."

"That's a very good thing for your father to teach you respect for your elders. As the good book says, there is an order to things. God is the head of man, and man should be the head of his household, and his children should give their parents the respect they deserve."

"Yes, and parents are not to provoke their children to wrath, right, Mr. Harper?"

"Very good, I see you're listening when you attend church services. I wish my son Jeffrey would listen to some of Pastor Whitman's sermons. That boy is so much into his friends right now that he wants nothing to do with church; I worry about him."

"Well, you have raised him up in the church. And doesn't it say that if you raise a child in the Lord, that when he is old, he won't depart from it?"

His face lit-up with surprise. "Wow son, you do know your Bible scriptures, don't you?"

"Yes sir. I like to read a lot and since we can't afford to buy many books, I end up reading the stories out of the Bible."

Mr. Harper looked towards the barn. "Well Luke…, I guess we better get started with our work for today. First of all, you can start with feeding the horses and then with cleaning out their stalls. In the back section of the property, there is an area where we dump the horse manure. There is a separate wheelbarrow around back that is specifically for the manure. Remember to put down new straw after you rake out the old. I also have a delivery coming in around ten this morning, so I'll need your help with that. This afternoon I would like for you to take one of the horses out for at least a thirty minute ride. Probably start with Spotty's Castle and then Lightning - those two haven't been ridden for about a month. Their owners mainly ride them in the spring and summer months, and since my son isn't into riding anymore, they are not getting the exercise they need. Now usually we ride them on that dirt road that runs adjacent to my property. That road leads to a few other ranches in the back hills. Or if you like, you can ride them in the meadowland of my property."

"Okay, no problem. Oh, one other question… Do the horses have their own separate saddle and tack?"

"Yes, as you probably saw in the storage room, each saddle sits on its own stand. The stands are labeled with each horse's name, and their bridles and other tack are right above each one. Now since Dusty and Sundance are mine, I only use the one saddle for the both of them. However, be careful with Dusty in the beginning…, it takes him a little while to get used to someone new. Make sure you get plenty acquainted with him first by giving him some sweet feed out of your hand. As you probably saw in the storage room, I have a gunnysack full of carrots, he loves those also."

"Okay, I think I got it. Now as far as the delivery, I don't have a watch on me so I'll try to keep my eyes and ears peeled for the truck when it comes in."

"If you don't happen to hear it, I'll come get you when it comes in."

Luke got right to work on feeding the horses. As he gave each horse an individual greeting, he came to the last one which was Sundance.

"Good morning, Sundance; how are you today?"

As if to respond, Sundance nodded her head up and down. Then she held a wide yawn and set her front leg forward, and stretched the sleep from her body. After filling her feeder with grain, and placing a leaf of alfalfa in her feeding trough, he began to clean out her stall.

"Well girl…, I have a very busy day today. I have all these stalls to clean out and a lot of other work to do. My father has always told me that hard work is good for you. He always says if you work up a good sweat, that it will clean out your pores or something like that. Anyway, I am doing this work because my dad wants our family to have a nice Christmas this year. You probably don't know what Christmas is, do you? Well Christmas is a time to celebrate joy and happiness in our lives. And the reason why we celebrate is because of Jesus being born. You see, he was born in a stable kind of like this. Well not exactly, but it was still a stable where animals lived. Now that might not seem like a very nice place for him to be born considering he was the Son of God; but he came humbly into this world. He wanted to show people that he was just like they were, just a human-being. But unfortunately the story gets kind of sad. He basically grows up alone, and then when he has some friends, one of them betrayed him and another one denied him three times. And even though he did many good things like feeding the poor and healing the sick, people got mad at him for speaking the truth, and they threw him out of their towns. So in the end, he basically died alone on a cross. You know up until now, I never thought of it that way; but he actually lived a very lonely life. Something else just occurred to me…; that maybe you feel that way too. You're mother died when you were young, and now Mr. Harper's son doesn't pay any attention to you anymore, so you feel all alone. I wish I could make all kinds of money to be able to buy you. I would take you home and care for you and love you. We would go on long rides together and maybe you would be happier with someone like me who would spend more time with you. I think myself that horses want to be ridden, like that is something that God places inside of them. Today I have to ride Spotty's Castle and then Lighting, but in a couple of days we will go out for a ride. Well, I have to take the wheelbarrow out and dump it, so I'll be right back. But before I go, I'm going to get you a special treat…, some carrots."

Entering the storage room he dipped a bucket into the sack of carrots and brought it over with him. Taking a handful of carrots, he opened his hand as Sundance began to eat them. However, after eating only a few, she stopped and reared her head back.

"What's wrong girl; you don't like the carrots?"

He opened his hand and showed her the carrots, but she reared her head back once more. Questioning why she had done that, he examined the carrots and saw the reason why.

"Oh wow, there's mold on these! No wonder you don't want to eat them, bad carrots will make you sick. Good Sundance, that's a good girl; you sensed something was wrong with them and didn't want to eat them."

He entered the storage room, and opened up the sack of carrots.

"Man..., a lot of these have gone bad, I don't think this sack of carrots is good anymore. I'll have to tell Mr. Harper about this."

He secured the bag of carrots, and proceeded to finish cleaning out Sundance's stall. Then next to hers was Dusty's, so he began to clean his as well. Once again he raked up all the manure and straw, taking many loads out to the back property. Each stall took approximately forty-five minutes to do each one. After he was done with Dusty's stall, he decided to take a little break and sat on an old wooden bench outside the back door of the horse stables. Looking out onto the back property, he thought of the coming day when he and Sundance would ride on those open plains. As he took a drink from a bottle of RC Cola to quench his thirst, Mr. Harper came around the corner.

"Luke..., taking a little break?"

"Yes sir. I was working up quite a sweat cleaning out the horse stalls."

"Well after you are done with your break, come help me with that delivery; it just arrived."

"Okay, I'll be right there. Oh by way..., I think the sack of carrots has gone bad. When I was giving some to Sundance, she didn't want to eat them. I examined the sack and saw they had mold on them."

"Really...? Well that just burns me up! I don't know how many times I have told that boy to make sure the feed is up to date. I guess

I'll put that on my list for the next order. Now…, did you give any carrots to the other horses?"

"No sir, only Sundance."

"Well, it's a good thing you started with her, because the other horses probably would have ate them. Sundance has a very keen sense of smell and can detect when something has gone bad."

As they made their way to the delivery truck, Luke questioned the obvious.

"You're son Jeffrey doesn't want to be doing this work anymore, does he?"

"No, and I guess it's time I came to grips with that fact. My wife and I love to run the feed and stables, and we hoped that one day Jeffrey would come to love it too. But I guess as they say…, it's just not his thing."

"Well you know Mr. Harper…, *it's my thing*. If after I work for you and I do a good job, do you think maybe I could work for you more permanent? I could come every morning to feed them, and come back in the afternoon when school lets out. Then on the weekends I can do the cleaning of their stalls and brushing them down and things."

"I don't know; that seems like a lot for a boy your age to take on. Are you sure your father and mother would want you to do that? Oh wait…; what am I thinking, you can't work for me."

"I can't?"

"No, the law states that you can only work during vacation time when school is out. The law prohibits youngsters from working during school time until you are sixteen years old."

Disappointment drew upon his face. "Oh…, I guess there goes that idea."

"And what idea was that?"

"Well the idea I had, kind of involves Sundance."

"So I'm guessing you were hoping to earn enough money to buy Sundance from me?"

"Yes sir, that's what I was hoping to do."

Mr. Harper held a knowing smile. "I see you have taken a real liking to Sundance, haven't you, son?"

"Yes sir."

"Well, I tell you what..., anytime you want to come over and ride her, you are welcome to, okay?"

"Okay."

As Luke gathered his work gloves, Mr. Harper could sense his disappointed about the horse.

"It's not the same, is it son?"

"What's that?"

"Just riding a horse, versus owning one - one to call your very own."

"No sir, it's not the same. It's like you develop this relationship with them. Horses seem like they really listen to you. I know you can talk to dogs and cats. But like our dog, I can be talking to her, when all of a sudden, she'll just take off. But horses stand there like they are really listening to you. Like when I talk to Sundance, it seems like she can pick up on what I'm feeling. And in a way, I feel like I can sense what she is feeling too. I feel like she just wants someone to truly love and care for her. She lost her mother at an early age, and I think she feels like she has no one. Especially since you told me that your son doesn't want to ride her anymore."

"Son..., horses are very expensive to keep and then of course there is the cost of buying one in the first place. Even if I gave your father a discount seeing we have known your family for years, we are still talking about eight-hundred dollars to buy Sundance. Then you have annual costs to keep her shod properly, and all the saddle and tack."

"I know, but that's why I wanted to be able to work for you to pay for all that stuff."

"Well, maybe something will come up in the future that will make it possible for you to own her."

"Yeah maybe..., I guess all I can do is hope and pray that something comes up."

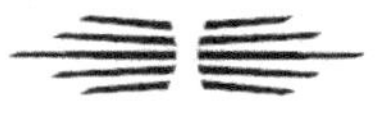

Chapter Three ~ Deck the Halls!

The morning broke as the Dawson family gathered around the kitchen table. Mrs. Dawson poured her husband some coffee and brought a pitcher of orange juice to the table before sitting down herself. She looked to the clock hanging above the doorway.

"Hun…, aren't you running a little late today?"

"No, actually we're not working today. The building inspector needs to come out to the job site to do an inspection, so I have the day off. However, I still have some work to do. Well, that's if the kids want to go looking for the perfect Christmas tree!"

Excitement beamed from Mattie's eyes. "Really…? Can we get our Christmas tree today?"

"We can if you like. I thought we could go on our traditional family outing of chopping down our own Christmas tree. Ben…, do you feel up to going out today to get the tree?"

"Sure Dad, I think I'm feeling up to it."

"Okay good, then it's all settled. After breakfast we will do our chores and then head out to Saunders Meadows to get the tree. I saw a beauty near the base of the foothills which would make for the perfect Christmas tree. Maybe we can also convince your mother to make us her famous pot roast with roasted potatoes for this evening's dinner."

"Is that a hint dear?" she questioned with a raised eye.

"Yes, not very subtle was it?"

"No, but that does sound like the perfect meal for this evening. However, if we're going to have that for dinner, I will need to stop at the grocery store to pick up a few items."

"That's fine; we'll all go into town later this afternoon."

Mr. Dawson observed his son sitting quietly. "Luke…, is there something wrong? You seem awfully quiet."

"No, I'm fine. It's just that I won't be able to go with you to get the tree. I have to go to work, remember?"

"I forgot about that. Maybe I can give Bob a call and see if he can give you the day off to enjoy it with the family."

"No, he needs me to be there. Yesterday we had a big shipment come in, and I still need to stack some of it in the storage room. Also, I have price labeling and the regular chores with the horses. Mr. Harper's son has already left on vacation and there really isn't anyone else to do it."

"Well I'm sorry, but I got the day off and I thought it would be the perfect time for us to get the tree."

"That's okay; you guys go ahead and have a good time. Besides, after a hard day's work, I'll have worked up quite an appetite for mom's pot roast."

Upon arriving from work that evening, Luke was greeted by Mattie who quickly met him at the door. Taking ahold of his hand, she hurried him along.

"Luke, come see…! Come see….! Come look at the beautiful Christmas tree we got!"

He walked in to see a large Douglas-Fir standing majestically in his living room; the fullness of its branches shrinking their modest sized living room.

"Hey, that's a really nice tree and a big one too."

"Yeah, mommy and daddy and me and Benny went and got it. We saw some other ones, but this one was the best. Then daddy cut it down and we brought it back to the house. We also went into town to get some food at the grocery store. Then after dinner, mommy said we can get the decorations out of the loft and decorate the tree. Daddy said I get to put the star on top of the tree this year. He said I'm big enough now and he's going to help me up the ladder to do it."

"That's good Mattie; I'm looking forward to it. We also need to find the Christmas records so we can have Christmas music playing while we trim the tree. Let me get changed out of these work clothes and we can try to find the records."

Overhearing their conversation, Mrs. Dawson walked into the living room; wiping her hands on her apron.

"Luke, Mattie…, dinner is just about ready so you need to get washed up. You can find those records after we eat. Luke…, go tell Ben that we are about to have dinner, I think he's in his room."

"Okay, I will."

Luke entered the room, to find Ben lying on his bed reading a magazine.

"Whatcha reading there, Benny?"

"It's an issue of Sports Illustrated that my friend Andy gave to me last Friday. But check it out..., the cover is for the football playoff preview, but inside, it's really the swimsuit issue," saying it with a raised his eye and a little smile on his face.

"Really, let me see!"

Luke flipped through the pages of the magazine, and then handed it back to his brother.

"You better not let Mom or Dad catch you with that, or you're a dead man!"

As soon as the words left his lips it reminded him of Ben's serious condition; and he wished he had not used those particular words. Ben then refocused his attention on the images inside the magazine, but his mind was elsewhere. Then to Luke's surprise, he began to open up about things in his life, which up until that time, he had never brought up before.

"You know something Luke; I never got a chance to kiss a girl," regret stemming from his voice.

"I thought you kissed that one girl Teri last year?"

"No, I only got to hold her hand; we didn't do anything else."

"Well don't worry, you will."

"Luke, I know what my condition is and how long they say I might have left. As I look at these beautiful girls in this magazine, it just reminds me that I never got to experience so many things in life."

Luke placed a caring hand on his shoulder. "Benny, don't say that, you'll be alright, you'll see."

"Thanks for saying that, but I know what the deal is. I'm just letting you know as your brother that I wished there could have been more time for us to hang out. I always hoped that when you got into high school with me, we could go on double-dates with some pretty girls and have some fun."

"Well, I don't believe everything the doctors say, besides, a lot of times they're wrong. I think in the future you will get to kiss a girl.

Maybe they won't be as beautiful as these swimsuit models, but not as ugly as the Wheeler's pug either."

Ben half-laughed. "Yeah tell me about it, that dog could scare himself in a mirror!"

Hearing their laughter, Mrs. Dawson yelled from the kitchen.

"Ben..., Luke...! Stop playing around and get ready for dinner!"

Hearing her voice, Ben quickly hid the magazine beneath his mattress as the two of them headed towards the door.

"Hey Luke, speaking of the Wheeler's and girls..., is there anything happening there between you and Carrie? It seems like maybe she has a crush on you."

"Really, why do you say that?"

"Man, are you blind or something? She sits really close to you on the bus, and she is always talking with you after school."

"I know, but we're neighbors."

"Hey man, you're getting to an age where you're going to have to pay more attention to some of these signs. Hey you never know, Carrie could end up being the love of your life."

"I already have a girl who is the love of my life."

Curiosity ran across Ben's face. "What girl is that?"

"Sundance..."

"A horse...? You're in love with a horse...? That's just crazy," shaking his head.

"It's not crazy. I remember when we had that one puppy named Ranger. You were all in love with that dog cuddling it all the time and taking it for walks, remember?"

"Well, yeah, but that was a puppy, this is a horse."

"So..., Sundance and I have a special relationship."

"A special relationship...? Now that's just weird."

"No, I didn't mean it like that dummy; I meant we have developed this close bond. Like when I'm talking with her and brushing her down, I feel like we understand each other."

"I don't know about you Luke; talking with horses. Next you'll be telling me that this horse talks back to you - like Mr. Ed."

Luke rolled his eyes. "Ha-ha, very funny."

"Anyway, speaking of animals, we better get to the kitchen before mom has a cow."

As they settled in for dinner, Mrs. Dawson went to the stove and pulled out a large serving tray of piping hot roasted potatoes to go along with her famous pot roast. As they all began to add their side dishes, Mrs. Dawson looked around the table.

"Luke…, how about you? Why don't you say grace this evening?"

"Okay, let's all bow our heads. Lord…, we thank you for the food that we are about to eat. I also want to say a special prayer for Ben and his health to let him be alright. We know you can do miracles, and we pray that you bring one into our lives. I also want to say a special prayer for all the animals in the world. I pray that you will bring someone into their lives who will truly love them. Animals need love too. Amen…"

Everyone said Amen, as Ben just shook his head thinking how his brother was taking this whole "loving animal's thing" a little too far. Then Mr. Dawson, sitting at the head of the table, directed a question to Luke in a firm tone.

"Well speaking of animals…, did you happen to feed *our animals* when you got home this afternoon?"

His father's tone sent a jolt of fear to run through him.

"I sorry Dad, I forgot. I know you fed them for me this morning, but I forgot this afternoon. Do you want me to go feed them right now, or after I eat?"

"I already got them for you, son."

He swallowed his emotions. "I'm sorry Dad; I'll try to remember next time."

"That's okay, I'm not mad at you. I just don't want you to get too wrapped up in this job that you forget about your chores around here."

"No sir, I won't."

Mattie, who was waiting patiently, finally saw her opportunity to speak.

"Guess what Luke…; you don't have to do the Christmas play anymore."

"I don't."

"No, Bobby Wheeler is going to do it."

"Really…, how did that happen?"

"Because Sister Anderson asked me if you were going to be in the play. Carrie Wheeler was there because her mommy is like the secretary lady for the church. That's when I told Sister Anderson that you got mad at me for saying you were going to do it. When Carrie heard you didn't want to do the play, she told her brother Bobby to do it. So now you don't have to do the play…, is that better?"

With a warm smile, he caringly ran his hand across the back of her head.

"Yes, that's better Mattie; thank you for doing that. But I'm wondering why Carrie would get involved in all that?"

Ben looked to his brother with a telling look. "See…, that's one of those little signs I told you to watch out for."

Luke looked off to the side thinking about his brother's statement - and smiled.

After everyone was finished with dinner, it was time to deck the halls and trim the tree! Mr. Dawson went to the back porch and grabbed a ladder to climb into the loft. One by one he handed Luke each box that had "Christmas stuff" written on it. Some of them were tree ornaments which were very old and fragile, so Mr. Dawson told him to handle the box with care. When all the decorations were brought down, they began to sort things out. Mrs. Dawson took a hold of one of the boxes and rummaged through it.

"Here are the decorations for around the windows and the garland to surround the fireplace. I'll begin by placing these things up first."

Mattie turned her attention towards Luke. "What about the music? The Christmas music..."

"Oh yeah I forgot. Mom…, do you know where those Christmas records are at? I want to play that one record that is transparent green with all the traditional Christmas songs on it."

Untangling the strand of garland, she drew a thought from the corner of her eye.

"I believe that record is stuck in behind some of your father's country albums in the stereo. I think behind his Andy Williams records."

Making his way to the stereo, he lifted the lid to search for the one he wanted. To the side of the turntable, was an area to hold the records. Going through them one by one, he finally found what he was looking for.

"Here it is! I found the transparent-green colored Christmas record."

Luke secured the record in place, and flipped on the turntable. The scratch of the needle hitting the record caused the family to pause; waiting for those familiar Christmas melodies. As the first song began to play, which was Silent Night…, Mrs. Dawson began to sing along. Her smooth voice was so calming to the rest of the family; as everyone could hear the feeling coming from deep within her. As the last of her words, "sleep in heavenly peace" resonated with each member of the family, it was almost as if she was saying, "Sleep my children...; sleep in a heavenly peace." A peace where there is no sickness or pain, and where everyone was safe and secure in her loving arms. A peace she wished for Ben's life…; to sleep in heavenly peace. The mood quickly changed as the next song which began to play was, Deck the Halls! Everyone joined in and began to sing along. Mattie led the way singing above everyone else, just slightly off key, but with exuberant joy. Mrs. Dawson then arranged some pinecones on the strand of garland specifically made for the fireplace mantle. As Luke tried to help his father untangle the ball of Christmas lights, Mattie brought the box of stockings over to her mother.

"Mommy…, is it time to hang the stockings by the chimney with care?" as she cited a line from the famous story, T'was the Night before Christmas.

"In just in minute sweetie; wait until I get finished with the mantle first."

Reaching into the box and pulling out a particular stocking, she turned to her mother once more.

"Mommy, this one is my stocking. Do I hang it right there?" as she pointed to the first nail placed in the fireplace mantel.

"Well why don't we hang them according to our ages, okay? First it will be your fathers, and then mine, then Ben's, Luke's..., and last but not least, will be yours."

"Okay, that way Santa Claus can put the right things in them. Usually he brings daddy some razor blades for shaving. I don't want him to put those in my stocking, I want some candy!"

"Yes sweetie, I'm sure he will bring you some candy; but he will probably bring you some fruit and nuts too. He wants you to be a healthy girl and he doesn't want your teeth to get rotten."

"I know, an apple a day, keeps the dentist away..."

Hearing their conversation, Luke joined in. "Hey mom..., do you know who else likes apples?"

"You Luke..?"

"Well yes, but I was talking about Sundance."

"Sundance...?"

"Yes, she's one of the horses at Harper's stables. She likes both carrots and sliced apples."

Ben shook his head. "All horses like carrots and sliced apples, you dummy!"

"I know, but Sundance is the only one who hasn't tried to bite my fingers off when I feed her."

"Speaking of horses..." Mr. Dawson interjected. "Ben..., maybe you would like to go for a ride over at Bob's place since Luke is working for him. Luke can saddle-up the horses so you won't have to do any heavy lifting. Maybe a little fresh air and exercise will do you some good. Do you think you would like to do that?"

"Harold...!" Mrs. Dawson snapped. "The doctors told us he needs his rest. I don't want him using up his energy going riding - especially not during Christmas time."

"Sandi..., the boy should be having fun and doing things to enjoy his life. What do you want, for him to just sit around waiting..., waiting for..."

But before he finished that sentence, he stopped himself. Silence filled the air, as you could cut the tension with a knife. He hurried to the front door, grabbed his coat, and abruptly left with the slam of the door. Upon seeing that, the kids continued to work silently on the decorations. Mrs. Dawson went to the front door and took ahold of her winter jacket.

"Kids..., continue with what you're doing, I'll be right back, I need to talk to your father."

Exiting the house, she saw her husband near the corrals, and petting one of the steers across its head. Walking over, she stood next to him, as the vapors of her breath rolled in and out in the cold night air. Standing to his feet, he placed his arms across the top rail of the corral, and looked to the stars in the clear night sky.

"You know something honey..., Luke told me the other day that animals can make very good listeners. I have to agree with him on that."

"Why do you say that, Hun?"

"Well, I would never admit this to anyone but you, but when I come out here, I actually talk to them. I talk to them about my hopes and my fears. And if I had a bad day, I tell them about it. But when I think about the real reason I talk to animals instead of people, it's because I know they won't judge me. I can tell them the things pressing on my mind, and the animal just listens with a wag of its tail."

"I'm listening honey; I won't judge you," as she prompted him to open-up to her.

He exhaled a labored breath. "Sandi, it's hard for me. I'm supposed to be the strong one around here. I'm the man of the house."

"Harold, you are the strong one around here. But being a strong man on the outside, and caring about things on the inside, is two different things. No one said you have to be made of stone in your heart."

"Yes, I guess you're right. I just don't want you to think less of me if I show my emotions in front of you."

"Honey, I wouldn't think less of you, in fact I would think more of you. If you show your emotions, then I know you care about the things going on in our lives right now."

Mr. Dawson gathered his thoughts for a moment before continuing.

"Sandi..., Ben is dying and I can't do anything about it! I am so frustrated and at times I just want to blame God for this. We have one boy who is like a little Hercules and another who is getting weaker by the minute. I just don't understand why this is happening. Did we do something wrong? Are we being punished for something we did as to why this is happening to us?"

As his emotions ran deep, Sandi wrapped her loving arms around him.

"Honey, the other morning I was sitting there drinking a cup of coffee and was thinking the very same thing. Wondering what I did wrong, and thinking I must be a terrible mother for allowing this to happen. But right now when I was singing Silent Night, a voice came to me which gave me the answer. It said that life is so temporal and we are just passing through. The time we spend here on this earth is so short in comparison to an eternity in heaven. Yes, we all wish we could live a full life here on earth, but what matters most, is what we do with the time we have. Right now I got upset when you wanted Ben to go riding. The reason I got upset, was my motherly instinct kicked-in and I got afraid for him. But you know..., you were right. Ben should be enjoying his life and doing all the things he wants to do with the time he has left. That's why I want you to get him that gift we talked about the other day. I think he needs it in his life right now. Another thought which came to mind, was the thought that we need to rest in the knowledge that there's a better place that awaits us. It gave me this comfort to know that if Ben's life ends sooner than later, then at least he will be in a place of peace..., a heavenly peace."

A smile creased his lips with a sense of resolve. "Come on Sandi, let's go back inside. Let's make this the most memorable Christmas ever as we share it with our children - for times like these are far too few."

When the Dawson's returned, Luke and his father finished placing the strands of lights and garland around the tree. Mattie searched inside one of the boxes to find a bag full of candy-canes.

"Daddy..., what about these candy-canes? Don't we put these on the branches too?"

"Yes sweetie, we will put those on just as soon as Luke and I finish with the lights and garland. Do you know the story of what the candy-cane represents?"

"No, I just know that I like to eat them!"

He smiled. "Yes, I know you like to eat them, but there is a story about the candy-cane. I think your mother has a poem about that; don't you honey?"

She lifted her head to the sound of her name. "What's that Harold? I was busy and I didn't hear what you said."

"Don't you have a poem about the true meaning of the candy-cane? I want Mattie to know what it represents."

"Oh yes…, in fact I think that poem is in the box along with the manger scene. If we can find that box, I believe I placed it in there."

Rummaging through the boxes, she found what she was looking for.

"Here it is. Mattie…, come over here. I want you to listen to this poem. It tells the story of what the candy-cane is all about."

"Okay mommy."

Mattie sat on the couch, as the others stopped what they were doing to listen as well.

A candy-cane hangs on the branch of a tree…, a symbol of love and his caring for me

Shaped like a "J" for his wonderful name…, the Father, the Son, the three in the same

Its color is white like the new driven snow…, born of a virgin so meekly and low

The color of red on the side of the cane…, is the stripes that he bore for our sin and our shame

In the form of a staff, the good shepherd is he…, watching his flock, he guards you and me

Its nature is strong, its taste it is sweet…, his power, his grace; his mercy runs deep

A candy-can hangs on the branch of a tree…, a symbol of hope, for you and for me…

As Mrs. Dawson finished, Mattie gazed at the candy-cane within her hands. With her new found knowledge of what it represents, she smiled, and gently placed the cane on one of its branches. Mr. Dawson walked over to one of the boxes, and took out a particular item.

"Here Mattie…, I have something else you can place on the tree."

Her face beamed with excitement. "It's the star!"

"Yes it is. Are you ready to place it on top of the tree?"

"Yes, I'm ready…, really ready!"

"Okay good. Let me get the ladder and I'll hold on to you while you place it on top of the tree."

He returned with the ladder, and he positioned it next to the tree. Mattie cautiously climbed the ladder, with her father supporting the small of her back for security. Then she took the star and gently placed it on the top branch. As the rest of the family applauded her efforts, Mattie stood wide-eyed and proud of her accomplishment.

"I did it…! I did a good job, huh daddy?"

"Yes sweetie, you did a very good job. Now why don't you help mommy with placing the ornaments on the tree?"

"Okay…, me and mommy are going to make the tree all pretty!"

Mr. Dawson then went into the kitchen to get a cup of coffee, returned, and sat down in his comfy recliner. Meanwhile Luke was busy placing the hooks on the ornaments, and handed each one to his mother, Ben and Mattie. As the songs on the record player continued to play in the background, the family cat, "Charcoal," named because of her fluffy charcoal coat…, came into the room and eyed the tree. As the cat cautiously approached the tree, smelling its branches; Mr. Dawson made his observations with a humorous overtone.

"Uh oh…, looks like someone has spotted the tree. It won't be too long before Charcoal bats a couple of those ornaments on the floor."

No sooner had he said that, when the cat went under the tree looking at all the shiny ornaments hanging on the bottom branches. Then playfully turning on her back, she began to bat one of the ornaments with her paw; like a boxer working a speed bag.

Mattie took notice of the cat's actions. "Look daddy…, Charcoal likes to play with the ornaments!"

"She sure does. It won't be too long before a couple of them will be on the floor."

Seeing the reflection of the lights in the face of the ornaments, Charcoal's eyes grew large, when suddenly; she went into a frenzy running all over the house wildly.

Mattie's eyes filled with wonder to the cat's behavior. "Daddy, what's wrong with Charcoal, why is she doing that?"

"I don't know. Maybe all the lights on the tree are a little too much for her. Or perhaps..., she is just filled with Christmas joy."

Contentment filled her smile. "Yeah, that's it; she must be filled with Christmas joy, just like us..., right daddy?"

Harold looked to his wife with an acknowledging smile of their earlier conversation. For times like these were *truly...*, far too few.

Hearing their conversation, Luke spoke up. "Speaking of Christmas joy..., how about I read the Christmas story this year."

Walking over to one of the lamp tables, he opened the drawer and took out a Bible, and brought it over with him. In preparation for the story, Mattie climbed on the couch between her mother and father and snuggled between them. With the sounds of a crackling fire in the background, they all sat quietly waiting for Luke to begin reading. Charcoal..., now settled down for her earlier frenzy, sat at base of the couch near Ben's feet, as if waiting to hear the story also. Then Luke stood poised to read the Christmas story.

"I'm now going to read out of the book of Luke - my namesake," he said proudly.

> *And it came to pass in those days, that there went out a decree from Caesar Augustus that all the world should be taxed. And all went to be taxed, every one into his own city. And Joseph also went up from Galilee, out of the city of Nazareth, into Judaea, unto the city of David, which is called Bethlehem; (because he was of the house and lineage of David:) To be taxed with Mary his espoused wife, being great with child. And so it was that while they were there, the days were accomplished that she should be delivered. And she brought forth her firstborn son, and wrapped him in swaddling clothes, and laid him in a manger; because there was no room for them in the inn. And there were in the same country shepherds*

abiding in the field, keeping watch over their flock by night. And, lo, the angel of the Lord came upon them, and the glory of the Lord shone round about them: and they were sore afraid. And the angel said unto them, Fear not: for, behold, I bring you good tidings of great joy, which shall be to all people. For unto you is born this day in the city of David, a Savior, which is Christ the Lord. And this shall be a sign unto you; ye shall find the babe wrapped in swaddling clothes, lying in a manger. And suddenly there was with the angel a multitude of the heavenly host praising God, and saying, Glory to God in the highest, and on earth peace, good will toward men.

—Luke 2:1-14

Chapter Four ~ The Parable of the Vineyard

At sunrise, Luke finished his breakfast and entered the living room to see his father reading the local newspaper. Upon seeing Luke enter the room, he promptly closed his newspaper and rose to his feet.

"Are you ready to go, son? I already fed the animals for you this morning so you wouldn't have to. I want to go into work early this morning, so I need to drop you off at Harper's a little earlier. I also want to talk to Bob about a couple of things."

"Okay, just let me get my work gloves and I'll be ready to go."

Luke grabbed his gloves and his coat, as he and his father headed out to Harper's. Upon arrival, Luke greeted Mr. Harper with a firm handshake and right away went into the storefront to get right to work. As he was tending to his duties, Mr. Dawson stayed talking with Bob Harper for a few minutes.

"So Bob…, how is Luke doing?"

"Very well. He's a very good worker and a strong young man for his age."

"Good, I just wanted to make sure he is doing a good job for you. Now in regards to what we talked about before, is it still going to be alright if you pay him his two weeks wages on Friday? Like I mentioned, financially we are in a bad way, and basically it's Luke's wages that is going to give us any kind of Christmas this year."

"Yes, I have no doubt he will continue to do a good job for me even if I pay him in advance. Actually, he asked me if he could work for me on a permanent basis. He wanted to work before and after school and on the weekends. That would have been fine with me, but as you know because of labor laws, I can't do that."

"So he wanted to continue to work for you?"

"Yes, I think he had something in mind he would like to buy with the money he would make."

"And what is that?"

"Sundance…; one of my horses."

"One of your horses?"

"Yes, he has developed this bond or a friendship so to speak with her."

"I see… You know Bob; now that you bring up the subject about horses, I wanted to talk to you about possibly purchasing one. I was wondering if you need any work done around your house. For instance…, like maybe some roofing or remodeling work in exchange for one of your horses."

"Well, the wife has been bugging me to build her a deck out back for family gatherings, so maybe we could work something out there."

"Bob…, once again I'm going to ask for a special favor. You know what kind of man I am, that I'm a man of my word. As you know, I wouldn't be able to start to build that deck until the spring, so I was wondering if you could see to give me an advance. I would like to be able to give the horse as a special surprise for someone this Christmas."

"Harold…, when I was having financial problems some years back, you and your wife were so generous to come over and provide our family with many meals until we got on our feet. You also helped me put up many fencing posts when I first moved here, and you have been right good neighbors to us. So as far as advancing you the horse, yes, I would be willing to do that. Now we are talking about Sundance aren't we? Because Dusty can be a little skittish and so Sundance is the better riding horse, especially for youngsters."

"Yes, that horse will be fine. Now if possible, I would like the horse to be delivered to our house on Christmas morning. Now there's a very important reason why I'm doing this, which in light of what you told me earlier, I would appreciate if you can keep this a secret. I don't want Luke to know anything about this right now."

Bob reached out his hand with a firm handshake. "We have a deal. And as far as Luke is concerned, you're secret is safe with me."

Near the end of that conversation, Luke happened to be near the entrance of the doorway when he overheard his father and Mr. Harper's conversation. A slight smile grew on his face, as Luke quietly backed away from the doorway so they wouldn't know he was listening. After discussing a few details about the horse, Mr. Dawson drove off, as Bob entered the storefront to check on Luke.

"How are you doing, Luke?"

"Fine… I just finished labeling all the bags of grain, and I was just heading out to feed the horses."

Luke, thinking he knew what his father and Mr. Harper were talking about, or at least he hoped he did, tried to causally to find out a little more about what he overheard.

"So…, what were you and my dad talking about?"

"Nothing much, just about how well you are doing working for me."

"Well that's good to know. So was that it, just about me working for you?"

"Well, we did talk about your father building a deck for me in the spring, but that's about it."

"So you're going to pay my dad to build you a deck?"

"Yes, your father and I are working something out in regards to payment for that."

Seeing he wasn't getting anywhere trying to gather information, he changed the subject.

"Okay…, I guess I better get back to work. I think this afternoon I'm going to take Dusty and Sundance out for a ride. I can't wait to ride Sundance; she and I have become good friends. I really like Sundance," saying it in a hinting manner.

"Yes I know you like Sundance, son, but I want you to be careful, okay?"

"Be careful? I'm a pretty good rider, Mr. Harper; you don't have to worry about me getting hurt."

"Yes, I know you're a good rider; I saw how you handled Lightning yesterday with no problem. But that's not what I meant."

Luke lowered his brow in confusion. "Then what did you mean?"

"Just be careful, son. It's fine to form a bond with an animal, but sometimes the things you hope for, don't always come in the way you plan."

"I'm sorry Mr. Harper, but I don't understand what you're saying."

"I'm just saying not to get too attached to any particular thing, because you never know how it might turn out. Anyway son, don't forget to take your breaks. I noticed you cut your lunch hour short yesterday. I want you to make sure you take your full lunch hour. Actually, the misses and I are going to have grilled-ham and cheese sandwiches for lunch, so I want you to come eat with us today."

"Okay thank you; ham and cheese sounds pretty good."

After lunch, Luke mounted his saddle, and took Dusty out for a ride. At first he resisted like Mr. Harper had told him, but then he seemed to settle down and enjoy being taken out. Then it was time to ride Sundance. Upon entering the storage room, Luke gathered her bridle and pad which was separate from Dusty's. When Sundance saw Luke coming with the bridle and pad, she immediately stood straight and tall; almost as if to show Luke she would be so proud to have him riding on top of her. Luke dabbed a little honey on the bit, which makes it easier for the horse to accept it in its mouth. Luke proceeded to lay the pad and saddle on top of her. Once again standing straight and sure, Sundance did not even flinch as Luke gathered the straps from underneath, and cinched her up tight. Leading her out of the barn, they walked out proudly as if making their way to the starting gate at the Kentucky Derby.

"Are you ready to go for a ride girl?" he said patting her neck firmly.

Talking a hold of the saddle horn, he pulled himself up. Then slightly adjusting her footing to compensate for Luke's weight, she stood poised and ready for his command.

"Okay girl…, first we will just walk out until we get past the last corral. Then I'll let you out, and you can run at your own pace."

With a gentle kick to her sides, while making an audible clicking sound, she began to walk down the trail with a proud gait. Once past the last corral he called out "Yah…!" and immediately Sundance bolted forward with a quick burst of speed. As the two settled in unison, horse and rider…, Luke let her run at her own pace allowing her to settle into a smooth stride. Then without a single command, he crouched deeper in the saddle and leaned forward. As if to read his mind, she surged forward at top speed, leaving a plume of dust behind them. As the wind brushed across his face, he could feel a surge of energy run through his body like he never felt before. It was almost as if Sundance was the power-source, and he was the conductor that gathered the pulse between them. The moment was overwhelming as his emotions ran over; bringing a tear to trickle down his cheek.

Oh Lord, this is so incredible! How could simply riding a horse, bring me so much joy! I have ridden many other horses before, but none like her. It's as if we were made for each other, and we can read each other's mind. Oh Lord, if I could only receive a gift like Sundance this Christmas, it would be the best gift of all!

After running at that high pace, he sensed she was ready for a breather; so he pulled back on the reins bringing her back down to a walk. Wanting to give his approval for her efforts, he patted her neck warmly.

"Good girl Sundance; I can't believe how fast you are. I know you are supposed to be fast in the quarter mile because you're a Quarter-horse, but man…, we were just flying!"

As they continued down the trail, he looked to the beautiful scenery around him. Tall pines majestically reaching to the sky set the backdrop to wide-open meadows of scattered oaks, maple and ash. The leaves which had fallen with the coming of fall, blanketed the ground in a colorful array, reminding Luke of the patchwork quilts his grandmother used to make. After continuing to ride a ways, he noticed the road split in two different directions. Wanting to take the bigger one, he adjusted the reins so Sundance would take the road to the right. As they headed down the road, he drew in a breath of fresh air and noticed the scent of a wood burning fire - apparently from the chimney of one of the local ranches. He stretched out his arms in contentment reaching for the sky.

"Sundance…, what could be better than this?" as her ears twitched at the sound of her name. "I feel like I could ride like this forever, couldn't you? You know this morning I overheard my dad talking to Mr. Harper. I'm not sure, but my dad told Mr. Harper not to tell me something; that it was a secret. I don't want to get my hopes up, but what if the gift my parents are going to give me this Christmas, is you?

And maybe that's why my dad is having me work for Mr. Harper so I could get used to taking care of horses because I'm going to own one. Wouldn't that be something, to receive a Christmas gift like that, I mean you? Oh girl..., you have no idea how grateful I would be to have you; it would be like a dream come true!"

As they continued on their way, Luke noticed he was getting to a part of the road which he was not sure if it was Mr. Harper's land anymore. As he approached some unfamiliar fencing, he began to turn Sundance around to head back. Just then, a pickup-truck approached on the road from behind. Luke held Sundance in place waiting to see who was coming his way. As the truck pulled to the side of the road and the man began to get out, Luke recognized him from the other day. The man approached with a warm greeting.

"Good afternoon, young man."

"Good afternoon, sir. I thought I recognized you from the other day at Harpers; you were buying some dog food."

"Yes I was. My name is Ron Friedman, and you're Luke Dawson."

"Yes sir, I am."

He turned his attention, and eyed Sundance up and down.

"That's a beautiful horse you have there."

"Well, she's not mine, she's Mr. Harper's. But yes, she is beautiful."

Taking a step forward, Sundance began to smell Mr. Friedman by placing her nose to his chest. He allowed her to sniff him as a gesture to get acquainted.

He commented. "She's very friendly, isn't she?"

"Actually I was told by Mr. Harper that she wasn't that friendly until recently. But to me, she's a real sweetheart. Oh by the way Mr. Friedman..., am I on your land? I noticed the fencing was different, so I wasn't sure."

"Well actually, the road you're riding on is County land, so you can ride on it anytime you like. My place is up the road a ways; in that white two-story house over there," as he pointed it out in the far distance.

"Oh yes, now I see it. You have a lot of big oak trees out front."

"Yes, most of those trees are hundreds of years old."

"Well Mr. Friedman, I better get back. I've been out with Sundance pretty long and I still have other work to do."

"It was good seeing you again, Luke. By the way..., how is your brother doing?"

"Ben? I don't know; some days he seems fine and then the next, he's so sick."

"Well, tell him and your parents that my wife and I will be praying for him and your family."

"Thank you sir, Ben can definitely use all our prayers."

As Mr. Friedman was about to leave, Sundance took a step forward, and attempted to smell him once again before leaving.

Luke took notice with surprise. "Boy Mr. Friedman, she sure wants to smell you a lot."

"Yes, I noticed. Maybe I spilt some maple syrup on my shirt from this morning's breakfast; the sugar might be attracting her. Or perhaps I just stink to high-heaven and she thinks I'm a horse!" as he laughed at his own joke.

"Yes, that could be it. Well..., I mean the part about spilling maple syrup on your shirt, not the part about you stinking like a horse. Anyway Mr. Friedman, I'll see you later."

"Okay, Luke, have a nice ride back."

"Thank you. If I'm riding Sundance, then I know I will."

*****

During the rest of the week, Luke continued to do his job with diligence and pride; knowing he was helping out his family for the upcoming Christmas holiday. On the Friday before Christmas, Mr. Harper called Luke into the storefront after he finished his lunch.

"Luke..., I have something for you."

Entering the cash register, he drew something from beneath the drawer. He handed Luke an envelope that came along with a firm handshake.

"What's this, Mr. Harper?"

"It's your paycheck. I told your father I would pay you in advance, and so your two weeks wages are in that envelope. There is also a twenty-dollar bill as a bonus for your hard work."

"Really…? Thank you, that is so great! I wanted to be able to get some gifts for the family, and now I can."

"Well, I'll tell you what… Why don't I have my wife cover the store for the rest of this afternoon, and I can take you into town to do your Christmas shopping. I have some last minute shopping myself, so while I do that, you can buy the gifts for your family."

"Really…! That will work out perfectly! That way I can surprise them with their gifts on Christmas morning."

*****

A couple of days later it was Christmas Eve; and time for their church's annual Christmas Eve Service. After getting ready in their Sunday-best, the Dawson family drove to church. After greeting fellow church members in the foyer, they took their seats. The rest of the congregation filtered in to near capacity, and settled down in the pews as Pastor Whitman took to the pulpit. He opened with a brief word of prayer, and then he opened his bible and began reading a particular passage.

> *For the Kingdom of Heaven is like a man who was the master of a household, who went out early in the morning to hire laborers for his vineyard. When he had agreed with the laborers for a denarius a day, he sent them into his vineyard. He went out about the third hour, and saw others standing idle in the marketplace. To them he said, 'You also go into the vineyard, and whatever is right I will give you.' So they went their way. Again he went out about the sixth and the ninth hour, and did likewise. About the eleventh hour he went out, and found others standing idle. He said to them, 'Why do you stand here all day idle?' "They said to him, 'Because no one has hired us.' "He said to them, 'You also go into the vineyard, and you will receive whatever is right.' When evening had*

come, the lord of the vineyard said to his steward, 'Call the laborers and pay them their wages, beginning from the last to the first.' When those who were hired at about the eleventh hour came, they each received a denarius. When the first came, they supposed that they would receive more; and they likewise each received a denarius. When they received it, they murmured against the master of the household, saying, 'These last have spent one hour, and you have made them equal to us, who have borne the burden of the day and the scorching heat!' But he answered one of them, 'Friend, I am doing you no wrong. Didn't you agree with me for a denarius? Take that which is yours, and go your way. It is my desire to give to this last just as much as to you. Isn't it lawful for me to do what I want to with what I own? Or is your eye evil, because I am good?' So the last will be first, and the first last. For many are called, but few are chosen.

—Matthew 20:1-16

As Pastor Whitman finished reading this passage, the congregation looked at each other wondering what this parable had to do with Christmas. Pastor Whitman then began to preach that evening's sermon.

"Now…, all of you who have braved the cold are probably wondering why I opened this Christmas Eve service by reading this passage. Probably out of all the parables of the Bible, this is the one that people like the least. I say that because most people look at life as to what is fair in their own eyes. In fact, that is what most of the television commercials are all about. Getting the most expensive cars, keeping up with the Jones'…, and making sure you get your fair share. During this time of year, most of you probably watch the TV special called 'A Charlie Brown Christmas.' There is a part of the program where the younger sister of Charlie Brown is making out her Christmas list. Then she begins to tell her brother to write out all the toys she wants. In the end she tells Santa Claus that if it's too much trouble to follow her list, to just send her money…, tens and twenties.

When Charlie Brown hears this, he throws his hands in the air in disgust, saying that even his baby sister has become commercialized. Charlie Brown's sister then goes on to say, 'All I want is what I have coming to me..; all I want is my fair share.' You see..., that is what I want to talk to you about this evening. As we prepare for our Christmas celebrations, probably what is foremost on our minds, are the gifts we are going to receive. Whether you open your gifts this evening, or like in our home, we open one present at night and then the rest in the morning..., it's all about getting gifts. But getting gifts or getting 'your fair share' isn't what Christmas is supposed to be about. Right now I'm going to call up Judy Sanders to sing a song for you. I want you to listen to the lyrics of this song. Too many times we look at Christmas like it's all about receiving gifts. However, what Christmas is really about, is the gift we received from God when he gave us his son. Judy..., would you please come up and sing that song for us."

Judy Sanders made her way up to the microphone, as the lights dimmed to give some seriousness to the moment.

Verse 1...
♫... High above..., looking below...., in the town of Bethlehem, seeing his son had just been born.
Knowing the cause...., the reasons why...., knowing that the child he sent, would suffer the pain and have to die....
Chorus...
"Yet knowing this, he gave his gift, with an unconditional love...
Sending him, for all the world, from his place from up above...
The greatest gift, for everyone, lay in that manger made of hay...
The gift of his love..., was to give his son away...
Verse 2...
Wise men..., coming afar..., bringing gifts to worship him, being directed by the star
His perfect plan..., so freely to take..., love expressed throughout the world, but hurt by the sacrifice he made...
Chorus...
"Yet knowing this, he gave his gift, with an unconditional love...
Sending him, for all the world, from his place from up above...

The greatest gift, for everyone, lay in that manger made of hay…
The gift of his love…, was to give his son away…
Yes the gift of his love…, was to give his son away….♫

After the song finished, Pastor Whitman walked back up to the pulpit and continued with his sermon.

"When I opened my sermon with the reading of that scripture passage, I wanted to share two valuable lessons this parable is teaching. In the story, one of the workers agreed with the master of the household on a day's wage. The worker was probably thrilled to get to work that day. I'm sure he had a family to feed and bills to pay. And since he was starting first thing in the morning, he knew he was going to get a full day's wage. However, the master of the household knew he needed more workers to finish the job. So he called in others to work the vineyard…; some around noontime and others late in the afternoon. Yet when it came time for all of them to be paid, they all got the same amount of wage. One of the men, who had worked the entire day, got upset, and said that the master was not being fair. He felt he should have gotten more money because he worked longer than the rest of them. Then the master seeing he was upset, said to the man, 'didn't we agree upon a wage and I gave you the wage we agreed upon? And why are you looking at me like I am an evil man, because I choose to be good and generous to others?' As we apply this parable to our lives, everyone is always looking out for number one. We are always trying to make sure that we get just as much, or more than everyone else. And right now during the holiday season, you see it the most. Kids comparing the gifts they got with their brothers, sisters or friends…, complaining they didn't get as much as the others did. And I'm just not talking about kids, adults do it as well. First of all…, Christmas shouldn't be about the gifts we receive, but about appreciating the gift that was given to us. And just like that song which was sung tonight, Jesus was born into this world for a purpose. But his purpose wasn't so we could have this cute little Christmas story of the baby Jesus and the manger. It was to fulfill his purpose to die on a cross for our sins. That my friend's is what Christmas is really about. The main message of the parable of the vineyard is to teach us, that the gift of heaven will be given equally to everyone who accepts him. Whether you are someone who has worked for years and years in the ministry…, or that person who accepts him at the last hour on their death bed. Everyone will receive the same reward of being with the Lord in heaven. Now that is not to say your hard work goes unnoticed, or there are no rewards in heaven for your labor, because there are. The Bible says in Matthew 6:20, that by your works you are storing up treasures in heaven. And unlike material possessions which will break, rust or fade away, your treasures in heaven will last forever. Now…, there is a second lesson to be learned in this parable. It is the lesson, that God has a plan when he gives his gifts to the people of his choosing. For example…, you may see other Christians in the church being blessed from the Lord abundantly. And in those times, you may feel like they are receiving more from God than you are. But the one thing to remember is that God knows what their particular circumstances are. Maybe they are going through a rough time financially and God has blessed them with some extra money. You may think that God is favoring them, but that little extra can make a big difference in their lives. So this Christmas, be grateful for what you receive. You already have been given the greatest gift of all. All the rest…, is just an extra blessing."

After his sermon ended, Mattie and her Sunday school class performed their play called, "The Little Christmas Lamb" which was a real blessing to the congregation.

After the service was dismissed, Luke was making his way outside, when one of the deacons of the church approached him. This particular deacon was known to give words of wisdom or a "Word from God" from time to time. Brother Abrams placed a firm hand upon his shoulder.

"Luke Dawson…, I would like to have a few minutes of your time."

"Okay…, sure brother Abrams."

As they made their way to a private spot in the back row, Luke began to question the reason why.

Oh man, what did I do that brother Abrams wants to have a talk with me? Maybe it's my Ranger Scout group that I haven't been going to anymore. I guess I can use the excuse I have been working for Mr. Harper and that's why. But then that would be kind of lying and I don't want to lie to him, especially because they say that he is like a prophet that God reveals things to.

As they settled into their seats, Brother Abrams turned to face him with a pensive stare.

"Luke…"

"Yes sir."

"I have a word for you."

"You have a word for me?"

"Yes, I am being led to tell you…, that you are a pillar."

"I'm a pillar?"

"Yes you are."

Confusion crossed his face. "I'm sorry brother Abrams, but I don't understand what that means."

"Luke, there are two kinds of people in the church. There are those who are pillars, and those who are rafters."

"Pillars and rafters…?"

"Yes… As you know the body of Christ is made-up of many parts, right? Christ being the foundation, and we the congregation, the structure of the church. Within that, there are pillars and rafters. Pillars are those who are strong and don't waiver in their faith. When trials come into their lives, their first instinct is to stand fast. Then there are those who are the rafters. These people need to be supported in order to stand. However, when trials come their way, they lose their faith and they fall. This actually goes along with Pastor Whitman's sermon. Sometimes in life and even here at church, you may think that other people are being blessed more than you. For example…, you see a lot people stand up and give their testimonies of how God is blessing them, or has done these miraculous things in their lives. However many times, they are also the same ones who come down to the altar once a month to re-dedicate their lives back to the Lord because they have fallen. You see, God knows he needs to encourage them by giving them extra gifts, because they are weak and are not ready to stand on their own. The Bible says in John Chapter 20 that, 'blessed are they that have not seen, and yet have believed'. In other words, Christ was telling Thomas that the only reason he believed he had risen from the dead, was because he saw the nail scars in his hands. Just like doubting Thomas, there are many people in the church that need some kind of proof in order to continue to believe. However you are a pillar. Pillars stand strong and sure no matter what circumstances come into their lives. Their faith does not need to rely upon outward blessings; they stand in the knowledge of what they believe. I'm praying for you young Luke…, you are not only a physically strong young man, but strong in your faith. I don't know why I was led to tell you this, but perhaps there is coming a set of circumstances in which you are going to be tested. So stand firm in what you believe son, and the Lord will bless you."

Luke thanked brother Abrams for his talk with him. On the way home, he wondered if what brother Abrams told him was in preparation in the event his brother died. Or maybe there was going to be some other trial which he was going to need stand firm in what he believed.

Chapter Five ~ A White Christmas…

When the Dawson family arrived home from the Christmas Eve service, they changed into some comfortable clothing and met back in the living room for a few family traditions. First, they were going to watch some Christmas specials on TV. Then before going to bed, there would be a time for The Lighting Ceremony. This was when the family would all gather around the tree, and Mr. Dawson would light a candle. He would proceed to tell his family what he was thankful for, and then light the candle next to him, held by his wife. After giving her thanks, she would light Ben's candle and then to Luke and finally Mattie. After they all had an opportunity to give their thanks, they would blow out their candles; watching the vapors rise from the candlewicks. This symbolized that their prayers of thanks were ascending towards heaven.

Mr. Dawson placed more wood on the fire getting ready for the evenings events. Suddenly, they heard a knock on the door. Mattie's eyes grew large thinking perhaps it was Santa Claus.

"No daddy, don't answer it!" she said with great concern. "If it's Santa Claus, we're supposed to be in bed sleeping. Santa won't leave us our presents if we're not in our beds and dreaming of sugarplums dancing in our heads."

Seeing his daughters concern, he ran a caring hand across the back of her head for reassurance.

"Don't worry sweetie, Santa Claus never comes before midnight, so I think it's safe to answer the door."

Upon opening the front door, he found the Wheeler family standing in the doorway bearing a homemade Dutch-Apple pie under a checkered cooking cloth. He greeted them in.

"John, Caroline…, it's good to see you. Come on in out of the cold; it must be freezing out."

John and Caroline Wheeler, along with their three kids, James, Carrie, and Bobby…, came in with a shiver. Mr. Dawson took their coats, as Mrs. Dawson welcomed them in.

"Come on in and get warm by the fire. We didn't expect any visitors this evening, but we are so glad you came."

As they all settled in, James, who is Ben's age, greeted him and the two left to go into Ben's bedroom. Bobby tagged along with his older brother. The adults soon filtered into the kitchen to talk, while Carrie, seeing Luke sitting alone on the loveseat, took a seat next to him.

"Hi Luke…, Merry Christmas…"

"Oh hey Carrie…, Merry Christmas to you too."

As the two sat glancing at one another and then shyly turning away, Mattie approached while turning her attention towards Carrie.

"Carrie…, did you see me in the Christmas play at church tonight?"

"No, I'm sorry, Mattie; I didn't go this year. Some of our relatives were visiting us earlier today, so only my mom and Bobby went because he was in the play. Was it a good Christmas Eve service?"

"Yes, and we did our play and everyone liked it. Some people even cried because this one part is sad when the mean boy throws the little girls stuffed lamb across the room. It was the only gift she had to give, and he was mean and he threw it away."

At this point, Luke could tell that Mattie was going to continue with the rest of the entire story, so he redirected her to the TV.

"Mattie look…, Rudolph the Red Nosed Reindeer is about to start!"

"Oh, okay…, are you and Carrie going to watch it with me?"

"Maybe in a minute; but you go ahead."

Mattie made her way in front of the TV, as Luke and Carrie sat side by side on the loveseat. Feeling a little nervous because of what his brother had told him about Carrie perhaps liking him, he tried to think of something to say.

"So Carrie, are you having a nice Christmas?"

"Yes, so far. But we don't open our presents until tomorrow morning."

"We don't either. But as you can see by the few gifts under our tree, there isn't going to be many to open. My mom and dad don't have much money to buy gifts this year. Actually that's why I'm working at Harper's; to help them out this year."

"Yes I know; and that's very noble of you to help them out. But speaking of gifts..., I bought you something."

Pulling a small wrapped box from within her coat pocket, she handed him the gift. Immediately his face flushed with heat, knowing he did not get her anything in return.

"Carrie, why did you go and do something like that? I didn't get you anything for Christmas. And besides..., we have never given each other any gifts before."

"Don't get upset, Luke, Christmas is about giving, right? Doesn't it say that it is better to give than to receive?"

"I know, but I'm the one on the receiving end and I me feel dumb because I don't have anything to give you."

"Don't worry about it; I didn't expect you to get me anything. Besides, it's nothing really big or expensive. I saw it at the store and I thought of you, so I bought it. Open it up."

Luke tore off the wrapping paper and opened the box. When he looked inside, his face beamed with excitement, seeing it was a small bronze statue of a horse.

"Oh wow, it's a horse! This is really neat Carrie! And look, at the bottom of the base it says it's a quarter-horse. Quarter horses are my favorite; Sundance is a quarter-horse."

"Yes I know, I remembered you told me how you like quarter horses."

Gathering a thought, he stood up and headed for the coat rack.

"Come with me Carrie, I have something I want to tell you, but I want to do it outside in private."

Handing Carrie her coat, the two went outside into the cold night air.

"Carrie, why don't we just stand here next to the house? I was going to go for a walk, but it's getting awfully cold out."

"Yes, they say we might get a foot of snow overnight."

As they stood there shivering in the cold, Luke blew on his hands, as Carrie waited for Luke to begin.

"So Luke, you were going to tell me something?"

"Oh yeah..., well the reason why I wanted to talk to you in private, is I might be able to give you a gift also."

"What do you mean by that?"

"Well I'm not sure, but I overheard my dad talking to Mr. Harper. My dad told him to make sure I wouldn't find out about the thing they were talking about. Then Mr. Harper told my dad that his secret was safe with him. I'm not sure, but I think the gift my parents are going to give me this year, is Sundance!"

"Really…?"

"Yes, and if they do, then I'll take you for a ride and that will be my Christmas present to you. Well…, unless you want to ride her all on your own."

"Luke that is so neat, I'm really happy for you. I know how much you love horses. As far as riding the horse by myself, I think I would rather ride with you. What do I do, get in back of you and wrap my arms around you?"

"Yes, of course you would have to hold on to me. Why, is that a problem? You don't want to be putting your arms around me like that?"

"No, it's not a problem at all. I'm starting to grow up now - if you haven't noticed. So it's not like I think boys have cooties or anything."

"Okay good. Oh Carrie…, there's one more thing I wanted to do before we go in."

"What's that?"

Luke leaned over and gave her a soft little kiss on the cheek. Carrie blushed and smiled at the same time.

"Wow Luke, what was that for?"

"I don't know…, just kinda saying thanks for the bronze horse you gave me. But don't go reading into that too much. It's not like I'm asking you be my girlfriend or anything like that."

"Oh no, I'm not going to go thinking that. Besides…, Luke Dawson likes horses, not girls, right?"

"Well, last year girls were kind of yucky to me, but not so much anymore."

"So are you saying that I'm not yucky to you?"

"Yeah, I guess that's what I'm saying," he said with a smile.

"Well, I'm glad I'm not yucky to you. But we better get back in; it's getting really cold out."

"Okay, let's go in."

As Luke headed for the door with Carrie trailing behind, she touched her cheek with the palm of her hand. Her thoughts and dreams of the future of what that little kiss might bring.

One day Luke Dawson...., one day you're going to give me a real kiss. And when you do..., you're going to want to marry me!

*****

On Christmas morning, Luke awoke to the sound of Ben's alarm clock, as he stretched his arms above his head in anticipation of what the day would bring. Ben, placing his feet in his flannel-lined slippers, headed for the restroom, when he looked out the window.

"Hey Luke, it snowed! It looks like we're going to have a white Christmas after all! It must have started overnight, because it seems like there is about six-inches on the ground."

"Really..., let me see."

Gazing out the window he panned the surrounding landscape to see it transformed into a winter wonderland. As Ben went into the restroom, Luke placed his slippers on and headed down the hallway when his mother abruptly stopped him.

"Not yet, Luke; wait until your sister is ready. I want for everyone to be together so we can see Mattie's face when she sees what Santa Claus has brought her."

"Okay, I'll wait right here."

Just then Mattie came out of her room in a floor-length pajama. Filled with excitement, she stood in one spot, jumping up and down.

"Did he come, mommy? Did Santa Claus come?"

"Yes sweetie, he came. But just wait right there until everyone is ready. I want to be able to take some pictures when you first come in."

Luke picked her up and held her on his hip. He proposed a question to stir her excitement.

"Are you ready to see what Santa Claus brought you?"

"Yes, I'm ready..., really ready!"

"Okay good. But first I need to use the restroom, so after I get out, we can open our presents."

Ben exited the restroom as Luke went in. As they were waiting on him, Mr. Dawson anxiously glanced at an old wooden coo-coo clock above the fireplace to see what time it was. When Luke came out of the restroom, they stood in the hallway waiting to enter the living room. Luke however, stood behind Ben and Mattie not really thinking he was going to have a gift from "Santa Claus" under the tree. Perhaps there would be a note of the gift he hoped he would receive.

Mrs. Dawson gave the signal. "Okay kids, you can all come in now."

The first thing that stood-out under the tree was a big red bow on top of the roof of Mattie's Barbie Dream House. She quickly knelt down on her knees looking it over, full of excitement.

"Mommy, daddy..., I got it! I got it!"

"You sure did sweetie. Santa Claus brought you what you wanted."

"It's so beautiful, mommy! And look at all the rooms it has! I got it because I was a good girl, right daddy?"

"Yes sweetie, you were a very good girl this year. But who else do we thank for the gifts that Santa Claus gives us?"

"We thank God, right daddy? Because God is the one who gives Santa Claus the magic to bring the toys to the children all around the world."

"Very good Mattie. Yes, we thank God for those who work hard to be able to give us the gifts that we receive."

Mr. Dawson glanced over at Luke. For it was only because of Luke working at Harper's that they were able to get that gift for her. Luke gave an acknowledging smile in return, and watched his sister begin to play with joy and contentment. Then the attention focused to Ben, as he saw his name and a ribbon on top of a new stereo cassette player.

"Oh wow, this is so cool; a new stereo and it is has dual cassettes and everything! Thanks Mom, Dad... Oh, I mean I'm glad Santa Claus brought me this," saying that for Mattie's benefit.

"Yes Ben, Santa Claus knew you have wanted a new stereo for some time now," as she gave her son a little wink.

Luke stood back watching the smiles of appreciation on their faces. Mrs. Dawson sensing that Luke might feel left out, handed him a small box that had a blue ribbon wrapped around it. Looking down at the gift in his hands, his heart began to race, hoping there was a note inside saying he was being given the horse.

"Luke..., why don't you open your gift?" Mrs. Dawson urged.

"You want me to open this one right now? I thought maybe I would open mine last."

"Well okay, if you like. I see there is a present for me under the tree which I can open. We also have the gifts that Mattie made us and our stockings as well."

Upon hearing her mother, Mattie remembered about her gifts. She quickly ran under the tree, gathered the envelopes, and began to pass them out.

"Daddy..., this one is for you."

"Thank you, Mattie."

She continued down the line. "And here's one for you mommy..., and here is one for Ben..., and one for Luke."

Each member of the family began to open their cards which Mattie had made for them. After reading them, they passed around each other's cards to see what Mattie had written on each one.

"They're all beautiful. They're the prettiest cards I have ever seen. They are much better than store bought cards."

"Thank you, mommy. We worked hard on them all last week at school."

"I know, and I can tell you worked very hard on them. Thank you so much."

"You're welcome."

After they gave her a hug in appreciation, she skipped back over to her Barbie Dream House and began to play once more. Thinking about the proud look on Mattie's face to be able to give out gifts, Luke remembered about his gifts for the family as well. He left to the back porch, and he returned with a large box. Then one by one, he handed each member of the family a gift.

"Luke..., what's all this?" Mrs. Dawson questioned.

"I got all of you a little something. Mr. Harper gave me a twenty-dollar bonus because he said I was doing such a good job for him. Mom, why don't you open your gift first?"

She tore the wrapping paper off her gift, revealing a new coffee cup. The inscription read, "World's Greatest Mom."

"Thank you, Luke; I needed a new coffee cup. I also appreciate the sentiment that is written on the cup; thank you."

"Well, like we talked about the other morning, don't ever think you're not a great mom. To me…, you're the greatest."

His caring words touched her heart. She reached for a tissue on the coffee table to dry her welling eyes. Mr. Dawson proceeded to open his gift, which was a new hammer, as the handle on his old one had started to crack.

He placed a firm hand on Luke's shoulder. "Very good son, you know the brand I like, Stanley. Thank you."

"You're welcome, Dad."

Mattie was next, so she opened her gift to find a Pink Corvette for her Barbie Doll. Filled with excitement, she walked over and hugged him tight.

"Luke…, it's that pretty car you see in the Barbie TV commercials, thank you!"

"You're welcome. I thought if Santa Claus was going to get you that dream house, this car would go along with it. That way Barbie can drive up to her new house, in a new car."

Luke turned his attention to Ben. "Okay Ben, open my gift to you."

Ben took his gift which was in the form of an envelope, and opened it up. In it was an IOU for the gift he was being given. A puzzled expression grew on his face.

"Luke, is this note saying that I will be getting a year's supply of Sports Illustrated?"

"Yes… Since you are now into watching sports and stuff, I thought you might like a year's subscription of the magazine to read. You'll start to receive the first issue in January. I got half-off the original subscription price from a coupon in the one Andy gave you. And it's the complete year…; meaning you will be getting *all the issues*," as he gave his brother a certain look to their little secret.

"Man Luke, I don't know what to say. Now I feel bad because I didn't get you anything."

"That's okay; someone recently told me that it is better to give than to receive. Well, I know that's from the Bible, but seeing your faces right now, I have to agree with her."

Mr. Dawson reached under the tree and handed his wife the remaining gift.

"This last gift is for you, honey."

"Well thank you, Harold, but I thought we weren't going to get each other a gift this year."

"I know, but there was enough money left over to be able to get this for you."

As Mrs. Dawson unveiled her gift, her face lit-up with surprise.

"Oh my goodness; a coffee maker!"

"Yes, and it's the automatic drip kind like you see on TV. You know the one that is advertised by Joe DiMaggio. It has a timer so you can set it for the time you get up in the mornings."

"Oh honey, this is so perfect; thank you."

Luke interjected. "Hey Mom..., that's why I got you that new coffee cup, so it would go along with what Dad got you."

Mrs. Dawson thanked her husband with a kiss, and then glanced at the remaining gift within Luke's hand.

"Okay Luke, I guess you are last. You still have your gift to open."

Staring down at the gift, his heart began to race in anticipation of what he hoped it might be. He slowly untied the blue ribbon which was wrapped around a white jewelry box. A jewelry box which he thought he had seen before on his mother's dresser. He opened it up to find a piece of paper in it. As he opened the folded paper with both hands, he saw the words, IOU written at the top. Trying to contain his excitement, he read the rest. {IOU: Santa Claus owes you a brand new Smith Corona typewriter from Sears, which your mother and father have placed on lay-away.}

Seeing what was written on the note, disappointment draped across his face.

"This IOU is for a typewriter?"

"Yes it is," his mother replied. "I hope you don't get upset with me, but I happened to run across that journal book you have in your closet when I was doing some laundry. I only read it to see what it was, and I realized that you write little stories in it. Luke, they are very good. In fact, if it wasn't for Mattie coming into the room, I wanted to finish that story where the two brothers go on a hike and find a secret passageway through an old abandoned house. Anyway, since you like to write, we thought the perfect gift would be to give you a typewriter."

The perfect gift…? He thought. *The perfect gift would have been to receive Sundance as my Christmas present… that would have been the perfect gift.*

Although disappointed that the IOU was not for the horse, he graciously went and gave her a hug.

"Thanks, Mom; this is very nice. I'm sure it will come in handy one day, thank you."

"You're welcome, but it's from the both of us; your father and me."

Luke looked towards his father to see his reaction, but by this time his father had gone to the kitchen, staring out the window. Luke, wanting to know what his father truly thought about his gift, approached him with apprehension.

"Hey Dad, thank you for the gift of the typewriter, I appreciate it."

"No problem. So you like to write stories, huh?"

"Yes sir, I do."

"Then I guess we choose the right gift for you."

Immediately he turned and continued to look out the window. By his father's response, Luke felt he really didn't care for the idea of him writing, and that the gift was really his mother's idea.

After they went through their stockings, Mr. Dawson looked out the window once more and hurried over to his wife; whispering something in her ear. Heading to the coat rack, he quickly put on his jacket.

"Honey, I'm going out for a little fresh air, I'll be right back."

After a few minutes, you heard a trekking through the snow, but it sounded different than just Mr. Dawson's boots. Suddenly you heard a loud whinny coming from just outside of the house. Luke, knowing that familiar whinny, knew right away it was Sundance. The emotions of his earlier disappointment quickly lifted with the understanding that his gift was meant to be a surprise.

Oh my God..., they did get me Sundance after all! I can't believe it, this is so neat! I can't wait to see her, imagine that, my very own horse!

Mr. Dawson shouted from outside the house. "Ben…, Luke…, Mattie…, come on out here! There's something I want you all to see."

Luke grabbed his coat and headed out the door. Ben followed, as Mrs. Dawson helped Mattie button up her long winter coat. When they were all gathered outside the front door, Mr. Dawson stood before his family with Sundance standing by his side. With excitement growing in his voice, Mr. Dawson addressed his family.

"As Luke already knows, this horses' name is Sundance. This fine Christmas morning, someone is going to receive a very special gift."

With his father's words, Luke felt as if his heart would leap out of his chest. He began to take a step forward to receive his gift, when he was stopped mid-stride by his father turning his attention towards his brother.

"Ben…, come on over here, son."

Ben walked over to his father, who in turn handed him the reins to Sundance.

"Merry Christmas, son…., she's all yours."

Ben's face lit up and was overjoyed at being given the horse. However Luke stood there stunned, as his thoughts were filled with utter disbelief.

No not Ben...! How could my father give her to Ben? She's mine..., Sundance is mine!

As Ben and his father began to talk about the horse, Luke tried to fight back the tears welling inside. Swallowing the tears that began to trickle down his throat, he tried to stay strong. His mother knowing the situation walked over and placed a caring arm around his shoulder.

"I know this is hard, Luke, but your father thought it was best to give Ben the horse given the circumstances."

Luke nodded his head in acknowledgement of her statement not being able to say anything in return. For he knew that if he tried to speak, his voice would reveal the hurt he was feeling inside. Not wanting to show how deeply wounded he was, he turned and headed towards the barn. Then almost on cue as if to mirror what he was feeling inside, the sky darkened, and a cold wind began to blow. A light snow began to fall once more, as he only wished it was rain to mask the tears streaming down his face. As the cold winter wind passed through the hole in his wounded heart, Luke slowly made his way towards the barn. His mother called out to him.

"Luke, where are you going?"

He struggled to get out the words which fell heavy upon his lips.

"If we're going to be keeping a horse around here, I better set up another feeding trough."

As Luke began to set things up in the corral, he began to cry out to the Lord.

Why Lord...? I don't understand... I am the one who does all the work around here! I am the one who wanted a horse way more than Ben. Sundance and I have a friendship, I love her! I do all this work, and yet Ben gets the horse? This just isn't fair! I'm the one who deserves Sundance! I know I'll never stop believing in you Lord, but sometimes life is so hard to understand. And right now..., I don't understand any of this!

Just then, he was alerted by the sound of footsteps in the snow, and knew it was his father. Luke quickly wiped the tears from his eyes to try to cover the fact that he was crying. Taking ahold of a couple of leafs of hay; he placed them in the new feeding trough. His father came and stood by his side.

"Oh, hi Dad..."

"Son, come over here for a second and let's have a talk."

"Yes sir."

The two sat down on a stack of hay. Luke took hold of a strand of it in order to focus on that instead of looking straight at his father.

"Son, let me explain something to you. A few years back I had it in my mind to get Ben a horse. He really wanted one back then, but that was before he started to get sick. Then when you started to work for Bob and he told me how attached you got to that horse, I knew that was going to cause a problem. But son, I feel like your brother needs that horse in his life more than you do. I don't know all there is about his medical condition and unfortunately neither do the doctors. But I felt it would be good for him to have an interest and to get him some exercise. You see, once Ben started to get sick, your mother has babied him. She doesn't let him do physical activities and I never agreed with that. But since the doctors have told us that he needs his rest when he gets sick, I went along with it. What I am hoping to accomplish with giving him this horse is to get him out and about, and maybe, just maybe, his health will improve. I am hoping with exercise he will get stronger so maybe his body can fight off this illness he has. I know perhaps that may not make any medical sense, but I need to give it a try. But if his health doesn't improve and he continues to get worse, then I still want him to enjoy the rest of his life. I want your brother to smile like he did today when I gave him that horse. And if he only has so many months left to live, then I want them to be the best of his life. I know lately he hasn't been that much into horses like he used to, but I thought this might give him the inspiration to want to fight. It seems like lately he has just given up and accepted that he is going to die. I know this must be so hard for you to accept, but can you now understand why I gave Sundance to him?"

Luke recalled his talk with brother Abrams thinking perhaps this was what he was talking about. That this trial in his life was coming, and he would have to stand strong and be that pillar through this situation.

"Yes Dad, I understand why you gave Sundance to Ben. And Ben does deserve to have some happiness in his life - I understand that. I guess what I don't understand, is why me? Why am I the one who has to do all the work around here? And guess who is going to get stuck taking care of Sundance…, me. Ben can't do the physical work of cleaning out her pen and taking care of her. He's not even strong enough to place the saddle on top of her. So here I'm the one doing all this work for Mr. Harper, but what did I get out of it? What's in it for me? Dad, it's just not fair!"

Mr. Dawson paused for a moment; searching for the right words to ease his pain.

"Son…, why did you take that job at Harper's in the first place?"

"Why…? Because you asked me to help out, and I wanted to make it a nice Christmas for the whole family."

"Well, didn't you accomplish that? Didn't you get paid for the work you agreed to do?"

"Yes, I did."

"Son, do you remember last night's sermon? How Pastor Whitman started it off by reading that scripture passage on the parable of the vineyard? Well I believe that part of the sermon was specifically meant for you. God knew you would be going through this rough time in your life. But he cares about you so much, that he placed it in Pastor Whitman's mind to include that in part of his sermon; I truly believe that. You see…, what that passage is trying to say, is for all of us to appreciate our station in life. You agreed to work at Harpers to help out the family, and that's exactly what you got. But now that you think someone else got a little more than you, you are upset and saying that life is being unfair. And because I was the one who made that decision to give Sundance to Ben, then basically you're saying that I am being unfair. But you see, as the father of our household, I have to deal with all my children according to what I think is best for them. I also know what you can and cannot handle. Ben is weak; he needs things in his life to encourage him. But you, you are strong, and I knew you could handle this situation."

Luke recalled the words brother Abrams spoke to him - words so similar to his fathers.

"Yes Dad, I see what you're saying. And I know…, I'm the strong one, I'm a pillar."

"A pillar…?"

"Yes, brother Abrams had a talk with me. He said that I'm a pillar because I am strong, and that other people are rafters because they are weak and need to be held up. But the thing is Dad; once in a while, I need to be held up! I need someone to take care of me! And I'm trying daddy, I'm trying to be strong in front of you, but sometimes it's hard, it's just so hard…!" as the tears began to form in his eyes.

Confusion rose on his father's face. "Trying to be strong in front of me? Son, what are you talking about?"

"I know you want me to be strong and not be a baby and be all emotional, but I'm just a twelve year old boy!"

"Luke, is that what you think? That I want you to be strong all the time and not cry in front of me? Because if you do, I never intended to make you feel that way. Son, it's okay to cry. Just the other day your mother and I were discussing some things about Ben, and I cried."

"You did?"

"Yes, I cried at the thought of Ben being taken from our lives. Let me tell you something else. When brother Abrams was telling you to be a pillar, he meant a spiritual pillar. To be strong in your faith and not falter or waiver in what you believe as a Christian. He didn't mean that you have to be a pillar by not having emotions. In fact, that is a lesson that I'm just starting to learn myself. That it's okay to release your emotions when things happen in this life. Maybe I haven't been such a good example because I felt I needed to show my strength as the head of our household. But I'm starting to learn that it's okay to have emotions, and you're not less of a man if you do."

"Well, what about me writing stories? You didn't seem too thrilled that I like to write."

"Son…, when your mother told me she found those stories in your closet; I was the one who suggested we buy you a typewriter - that was my idea."

"Really…?"

"Yes it was."

"So you don't think that writing is dumb or sissy?"

"Don't ever think that anything you want to accomplish in this life is dumb. I want to support and encourage all my kids the best way I can."

Gathering his thoughts, a revelation came to mind. "So then basically what you're trying to tell me, is you feel you need to support and encourage Ben by giving him Sundance?"

"Yes, that's exactly what I'm telling you."

Luke placed his arms around his father and held him tight. Then he began to release the tears he was holding onto. Tears of forgiveness towards his father, as he now understood why he did not receive the gift he had longed for. His father ran a caring hand across his head, as Luke looked up to his loving father.

"Dad, I'm sorry I got upset with you for giving Sundance to Ben. I guess I was like that man in the parable of the vineyard. I got upset when I felt others got more than me."

"Son, let me tell you something that I've learned over the years. Hard work always brings about its own reward. Did you see the look on Mattie's face when she saw her doll house? And did you see that look of appreciation when your mother received her new coffee maker? And what about Ben..., Ben's face just lit-up when I gave him that horse. Son, one day you'll come to understand, that material things in life are so temporary, but the memories of the smiles on their faces will last you a lifetime. Luke..., this Christmas has been so great and it's because of you. You were the one who worked by the sweat of your brow so our family could enjoy this Christmas. You may not fully understand all of that right now..., but one day you will."

Luke smiled with appreciation. "Thanks Dad, thanks for having this talk with me. I feel a lot better about everything."

"You're welcome my son..., you're welcome."

Chapter Six ~ Hoofprints in the Snow…

After Luke and his father had their talk, they began to walk towards the house when they saw Ben bringing Sundance towards them.

"Can I go for a ride, Dad? I think I'm feeling strong enough to do it today."

"Well…, why don't you go inside the house and get something to eat first. You haven't had breakfast yet, and if you are going to ride today, you'll need all your strength. In the meantime, Luke and I will go over to Bob's place to pick up the saddle. Bob threw in the saddle for free as long as Luke comes by his place and rides Dusty to give him some exercise. Luke and I will stop at the local diner and grab a bite to eat on our way there. Tell your mother to make you some breakfast and then rest-up for a bit. When we get back, then we'll see about you going on that ride."

A couple hours later, Luke and his father returned from Harper's with the saddle. As they set-up the saddle and tack in the barn they noticed the weather was starting to get worse. The snow which started earlier as just a few flakes was now coming down hard in a blustering wind. After they placed the saddle in the barn, they began to make their way back to the house, when Ben came out to greet them.

"Okay, I'm ready to go for a ride."

"I don't know, Ben, this storm appears to be getting worse. Also, the temperatures are well below freezing right now. I don't think it's such a good idea to take her out."

Disappointment drew upon his face. "Ah come on Dad, please…? I really want to go for a ride today. I won't go too far, but I really want to do this."

Although it was against his better judgment, Mr. Dawson did not want to discourage his son from going on his ride. After all, that is what he wanted, for his son to get out and about for some physical exercise.

"Okay Ben, but just for a little while and then come right back. Luke will help you with the saddle. If you need any further help, just come and get me; I'll be in the house."

"Okay, thanks."

Luke and Ben began to get Sundance ready for the ride, when Sundance attempted to smell Ben on his chest and arms.

"Why is she doing that, Luke? Why is she trying to smell me like that?"

"I'm not sure. I have only seen her do that with one other person; that Mr. Friedman who lives in the back hills beyond Mr. Harper's place. Mr. Harper said that she has a keen sense of smell. He said she can detect when something is not right. I'm not sure what that means as far as her trying to smell you, but either way, at least she didn't try to bite you."

Ben half-laughed. "Yeah, I guess that's a good thing."

Luke placed the pad and saddle on top of Sundance. As he cinched her up tight, Ben turned to him with something on his mind.

"Luke..., I want to thank you for being so cool about this. I know you have wanted a horse for some time now. But I want you to know that even though Dad gave her to me, I want you think of her as yours also. Also knowing what my condition is and how much time I have left, she's probably going to yours pretty soon anyways."

"Ben, don't say that...; I hate it when you talk like that. You don't know, the doctors don't even know. They say you only have so many months left to live, but how do they know when they don't even know what's wrong with you. To me that just doesn't make any sense. That's like saying that one day a tire on Dad's pickup truck is going to blow out, but no one knows exactly when it will happen."

"Yes that's true; but you do know that tire is starting to go when you see how far the tread has worn down. The doctors can tell my tread is wearing thin." Luke brushed those thoughts aside; shaking off the notion of Ben dying.

Sundance was now ready to go, as Luke gave his brother a leg-up in the saddle. As Ben took a hold of the reins, Luke had a few instructions.

"Okay, start her out slow to get her warmed up first before letting her out. And don't kick her that hard, a slight one will do with your verbal command."

"I will, I've ridden a horse before you know. It's like that old saying; it's like riding a bike, you never forget. Or in this case…, it's like riding a horse!"

Laughing at his own joke, Ben began to cough uncontrollably. After continuing for a quite a while, Luke got seriously concerned as his brother seemed to have a hard time stopping.

"Are you okay, Benny? That doesn't sound too good."

"I'll be okay," coughing through his words. "I'll be alright..."

"You don't sound alright to me. I don't think it's such a good idea for you to ride today."

Now appearing weaker than ever before; Ben gave his brother a long telling look.

"Luke, I've coughed like this many times before and it's getting worse. There are other things that are starting to happen to me, but I don't want to alarm Mom and Dad. Luke, if I don't take this ride right now, I may never get a chance to ride again. So as your brother I'm asking you…, please…, let me have this ride."

His telling words pierced Luke to the core. Now realizing what his brother was really trying to tell him, he turned his attention towards Sundance.

"Okay Sundance, you be careful on those trails and watch out for any coyotes that may be out and about. That's my brother you have on top of you and I need for you to take good care of him. That's my brother and I love him very much."

Upon hearing his brothers caring words, Ben sent an appreciative smile, and then panned the surrounding landscape.

"Luke…, if I take a little longer on this ride, don't worry; okay? For today I want to ride like I have never ridden before. I want to ride with the wind in my face and to breathe the fresh mountain air… I want to see wide-open meadows and pine trees filled with fresh-fallen snow upon its branches… I want to follow a trail of rabbit prints in the snowy meadows, and to watch an eagle take flight and circle from high above… And as I ride, I want to laugh and raise my hands in triumphant freedom. For I know that this ride I take will be the ride I will always remember!"

Upon hearing his brother's triumphant declaration, Luke smiled through his tears to the understanding of what his brother really meant. As Luke stood at the edge of the corral watching his brother ride away, he waved goodbye bidding them a fond farewell.

"Take care of yourself Benny. And Sundance..., take him for a ride. A ride he'll remember for the rest of his life."

As the sun began to set, Luke labored in his thoughts at the passing of time. He peered out the window to see the snow flurries worsen, as anxiety grew within. He walked into the living room to see his parents playing with Mattie on the living room floor, as he anxiously stood before them.

"Mom, Dad..., I'm getting a little worried."

His mother casually looked up. "What are you worried about?"

"Ben..."

She perked up with interest. "Ben...? Why are you worried about Ben? Is he in the bathroom getting sick again?"

"No, he hasn't come back yet."

She quickly rose to her feet. "What...! What are you talking about? When you came in from feeding the dog, I thought he was with you?"

"No Mom, he's still out riding. He told me not to worry that he was going on a longer ride. I just didn't think he was going to stay out this late."

She rushed to the front door and opened it up. "Oh goodness Harold, it's practically a blizzard out; go find him!"

Mr. Dawson rose to his feet and hurried towards the phone. "Luke..., go get dressed in some warm clothing. I'm going to call Bob Harper and see if he can come over with his jeep. My truck doesn't have good ground clearance, so we won't get very far on those back trails with all this snow."

Luke hurried to change his clothes, when his father entered his room with a look of frustration.

"Stop Luke...; we're not going anywhere. Bob just told me they shut down Double-A Ranch Road because of the heavy snow. He said that everything is at a standstill right now. And because it's the holiday, the snow plows are not clearing the roads and they won't be out until tomorrow morning."

"Tomorrow morning! How are we going to find Ben if something happened to him?"

"Well, I hope he is currently on his way back right now, but if for some reason he gets lost, horses have a pretty good sense of direction. What Sundance will probably do, is she will either come back here, or make her way back to Bob's place because she is familiar with his ranch."

"But what if he got hurt and he can't make it back? Dad, this is all my fault! I never should have let him go. Ben was coughing really badly and he didn't look good. I shouldn't have let him go."

"This is not your fault. You're brother wanted to go for a ride and nothing was going to stop him - I could see it in his eyes."

"Yeah, I guess you're right; I saw it in his eyes too. Hey Dad, doesn't Bob have a snowmobile we can use to look for Ben?"

"Yes, as a matter of fact, I think he does. Let me give him another call to see if he is willing to drive it over here."

Mr. Dawson entered the kitchen to make the call, when he quickly hung up the phone.

"The phone is disconnected. The lines must be down because of the storm. Besides, in an hour it's going to be too dark to go looking for him anyways. Let's just hope Ben makes it back soon."

For the next couple of hours the Dawson family sat quietly in the living room. Only the sound of the crackling fire and the howling winds cut the silence as they kept a watchful eye on the clock. Finally around nine o'clock they were alerted by a sound near the front door. Luke rushed to the front window to take a look; only to be disappointed.

"It's just Misty; she's at the front door."

"Let her in and put her in the back porch. I don't know how that dog always seems to get out of the fence. I guess it's because she's part wolf. She is always digging those deep burrows in the ground."

Luke opened the door to see Misty wagging her tail and standing about a foot higher than normal because of the depth of the snow.

"Come with me, Misty, out to the porch," as he grabbed her collar and whisked her off.

Mrs. Dawson turned to her husband with a look of grave concern. "Harold, what do you think happened to him? Do you think he can survive out there in these freezing temperatures?"

"I don't know, honey. Maybe if he found some shelter to stay out of the wind. But with these snow conditions and the temperature well into the teens, it doesn't look too good."

Falling upon his shoulder, she burst into tears. "Oh Harold, why is this happening!"

He hugged her close to his side. "I don't know, honey; perhaps only God knows."

Knowing her husband so well, Mrs. Dawson could sense he had something on his mind.

"What is it, honey? I know you're thinking about something."

"Sandi, I know this is not what you want to hear right now; but maybe this is all for the best. Maybe if he goes this way, he won't have to go through all the pain and suffering as his condition gets worse."

"I know, and I can't say that I haven't thought of that. But I'm still praying; praying for God to move his hand upon this situation."

"Try to get some sleep, honey. We can't do anything until tomorrow morning anyway."

"Okay, maybe just for a couple of hours and then wake me up. We can trade off around three in the morning."

"Okay, I'll wake you."

*****

Into the morning hours, Mr. Dawson let his wife sleep-in. He began to prepare some coffee when Mrs. Dawson walked into the kitchen in her robe. She held a wide yawn and stretched her back.

"Why didn't you wake me?"

"You looked like you were in a deep sleep, so I let you rest," as he handed her a cup of coffee.

"Actually, I did sleep really well which is kind of surprising considering the situation. But for some reason, I woke up with a calming assurance. So is it still snowing out?"

"No, actually it looks like the storm has passed and when the sun rises, it looks like it's going to be a beautiful day."

"Is the phone still out?"

"It was about an hour ago, but I haven't tried it since."

Mr. Dawson headed towards the phone, when suddenly it rang.

"Well, I guess that answers that question," he commented reaching for the phone.

"Hello…"

As he listened intently to the caller, his voice filled with excitement.

"Yes..! Just as soon as I can get in touch with Bob Harper we'll be right over; this is great news!"

He hung-up the phone and he turned to his wife. "Honey, he's alright! Ben is alright!"

"He is?"

"Yes, that was old Doctor Friedman. He said that Ben showed up late last night at his place and collapsed in his front yard with Sundance. He took Ben into the house and has been taking care of him during the night. He said he wasn't able to contact us, because the phones were down."

She wrapped her arms around him and held him tight. "Oh thank God! Oh honey, do you think the roads are passable to make it over there?"

"Yes, I think the snow plows should be clearing the roads by now. I'll call Bob to let him know we will be going over. Then we'll take his jeep over to Doctor Friedman's house from there."

Hearing their conversation, Luke entered the kitchen. "Hey…, I thought I heard you guys say they found Ben. Is he alright?"

"Yes, Doctor Friedman found him. Apparently Ben found his way over to his house and he collapsed in his front yard with Sundance."

"Doctor Friedman…? You mean that older man Ron Friedman who lives way in the back hills past Mr. Harpers place?"

"Yes, that's *Doctor Friedman.* He used to be the town's doctor years ago. He used to practice before Doctor Jenkins came. You probably don't remember him because you were very young when he retired."

"And what about Sundance; did he say anything about her?"

"No, just that Sundance was with Ben when Doctor Friedman found him."

"So are we going over there to get Ben?"

"Yes, just as soon as I get ahold of Bob on the phone. We still need need to use his jeep to make it through those back roads."

When they arrived at Bob's house, they piled into the jeep and headed out to get Ben. Upon arriving at Mr. Friedman's house, he greeted them at the door. Luke rushed into the house and went to his brother's side.

"Hey Benny..., how-ya doing?"

"A little tired, but I'm doing pretty good. Mr. Friedman, or should I say Doctor Friedman, took really good care of me."

Just then Mr. Dawson came and hugged his son with a warm embrace.

"Ben, I'm so glad you're alright; your mother and I were worried sick."

"I know, Dad, and I'm sorry."

"So what happened anyway?"

"Well, as I was riding, I noticed that the storm started to get really bad. As I started to turn around, a pack of coyotes saw us and started to chase after us. Sundance got spooked and started running in an area I had never seen before. The coyotes stopped chasing us, but by that time, I was lost and didn't know how to get back. I started to feel really weak and dizzy as I tried to follow the trail of hoof tracks to find our way back. But when we got so far, new snow had fallen and I lost the trail. With the wind making it even colder, I must have passed out, because the next thing I knew, I was lying on the ground in the snow. I tried to get up, but I was so weak that I didn't have the strength to get back up on top of Sundance. I must have passed out again, because the next thing I knew, I was being dragged. I then realized that Sundance had taken ahold of the back of my shirt collar and was trying to pull me along. Seeing how hard she was struggling to help me, it seemed to give me the inner strength to climb back on top of her. From there, all I can remember is I was bent over the saddle trying not pass out again. I couldn't see ten feet in front of my face because of the heavy snow falling, but thank God, Sundance knew where she was going. The next thing I remember, I was lying on the ground in front of Doctor Friedman's house."

With Ben saying that, Luke's thoughts went to Sundance.

"Mr. Friedman…, where is Sundance, is she alright?

"I don't know, son; she ran off. After I tended to Ben, I went back outside to put her in the barn. The saddle had partly fallen off when Ben fell out. I unhitched the saddle and started to walk her to the barn, when suddenly, a tree-limb heavy with snow, fell and almost hit her. She got spooked and tried to pull away from me as I held on to the reins. I guess with it being so wet out, the bridle slipped off her head and she ran off. I'm sorry son, I tried."

A sense of urgency drew upon Luke's face. "Dad, we need to find her!"

"We will, but first let's get Ben back home. That's if Doctor Friedman thinks he is in good enough shape to travel."

Ben interjected. "Actually Dad, I'm more than good - I'm great!"

Seeing this burst of excitement, he questioned his response.

"How is that Ben, why did you say that you're great?"

"I'm great because I don't think I'm going to be dying anytime soon."

A look of shock rose upon his face. "What!"

"Yes, Doctor Friedman thinks he knows what my condition is."

Doctor Friedman turned to explain.

"Harold, I think your son has a condition called Addison's disease. It's a deficiency of the adrenal glands that don't produce glucocorticoid steroids in the system. I can't be one-hundred percent sure, but by all of his symptoms, I am almost positive that's what he has. Other doctors may not have been able to diagnose this disease, because unless you are familiar with its multiple symptoms, it is easily overlooked."

"So you mean to tell me that Ben is going to be alright; that there is a cure for what he has?"

"There's not a cure, but it is treatable by taking medications called hydrocortisones. If he does that, then he should live a normal healthy life."

His face beamed with joy and amazement. "Oh my God, this is incredible! So how did you know he had this particular disease?"

"Ben explained some of his symptoms to me and I was trying to piece it together. However, when I was checking out his vital signs and he pulled up his shirt, I noticed he had a scar on his rib area."

"Yes, Ben was climbing a tree when he was younger and he slipped and cut himself pretty deep on a branch."

"Well, when I saw the color of his scar, it was darker than normal. That is a symptom which is unique to Addison's. The pigmentation of scars will change in color and become dark. I asked him a few other questions, like if he craves salty foods. That's when he told me he puts extra salt on his food and eats a ton of sunflower seeds. Now, what I will be doing is writing up a summary of my diagnosis to Doctor Jenkins. Then he can run this particular test that will identify his condition for sure."

With sincere appreciation, Mr. Dawson shook his hand warmly.

"Doctor Friedman, I don't know how to thank you enough. Thank God you figured out what Ben has or he might have died."

Ben turned to his father in response. "Yes Dad, we should be thankful that Doctor Friedman figured out what I have. But I also think we need to be thankful that Sundance brought me here in the first place."

Bob, who was standing nearby, questioned about that. "Luke..., have you ever rode Sundance over here to Doctor Friedman's place?"

"No sir. Once I met up with Mr. Friedman on the road just past where your property ends, but I never rode all the way to his house. Why are you asking me about that?"

"Because it's just strange that Sundance would have brought Ben over here. Horses will return to those places that are familiar to them. She should have either gone back to your house, or over to my place. And seeing how you have to bypass my ranch in order to get to Doctor Freidman's place..., it's even stranger."

Thinking about Sundance being out in those winter conditions, Luke turned to his father with concern.

"Dad…, what about Sundance? It was awfully cold last night. Can she survive out there without any shelter?"

Mr. Dawson then turned to Bob for his expertise.

"Well Luke…, horses are pretty good at adapting to cold weather. However, it takes them time to do that. In other words, you are supposed to keep them in some kind of shelter so their bodies can adjust to the coming winter season. The thing I'm concerned about is that Sundance did not have that adjusting period. She went from a warm stall in my barn, to below freezing temperatures last night. Hopefully she was able to survive last night's storm."

After getting Ben into the Jeep, they all headed out, and came to the fork in the road towards Bob's place. Luke, keeping watch to see if he could see Sundance, spotted some tracks in the snow that looked like hoof prints. He pointed to the tracks with a sense of urgency.

"Dad, look! I think those are Sundance's hoof prints in the snow going out towards that open meadow I like to ride in sometimes."

"Okay, but let's get Ben back home first before we go out looking for her."

Ben interrupted. "No dad; let's try to find Sundance first, I'll be okay."

"Are you sure?"

"Yes, it's the least we can do. Sundance saved my life by taking me to Doctor Friedman's; so I think it's only right that we try to save hers."

"Okay, we'll head-on out to see if we can find her."

They journeyed for about a mile scanning the countryside for Sundance. Finally they came to a point where the trail ended near the base of the base of the foothills. Seeing the rough terrain ahead, Bob stopped the jeep.

"The trail ahead is too rough to continue. It's either on foot or on horseback from here on out."

Mr. Dawson added. "Yes Luke, let's take Ben home first and then we can come back later to look for Sundance."

Luke answered with firm resolve. "Oh alright, but I'm coming right back to try to find her."

Bob interjected. "No Luke, *we'll* come back to try to find her. When we get back to my place, we'll saddle up Captain Morgan and Dusty. Horses identify each other through their sense of smell. Dusty and Sundance are close, so I'm hoping that Dusty might lead us to her."

As they journey back to the main road leading to Bob's ranch, Luke spotted something in the far distance.

"Wait Mr. Harper! I think I see something way out there near those big boulders."

Bob brought the vehicle to a stop, and stood on the step-side of the jeep to take a look.

"It's something alright, but if it's Sundance she's down and that's not good."

The fear of the impending question resonated in Luke's voice. "What do you mean by that Mr. Harper?"

"Well if she's down, then that means she might be hurt. And if she got hurt, then she wouldn't be able to keep her body temperature up during the night. You see, horses will move around to raise their body temperatures in severe cold. Luke..., you and I will hike on out there. Your father can stay in the jeep with Ben."

"No," Ben answered firmly. "I want to go with you."

"Are you sure you're strong enough to be walking in the snow?"

"Yes, I'll be fine."

"Okay, then we will all go out there."

As they made their way trekking through the snowy meadow, they saw more hoof prints in the snow and began to follow them. As they drew closer to the group of large boulders, their fears were confirmed as they realized it was a horse lying on its side. Luke hurried his pace as his thought's raced along with his beating heart.

Oh God, please don't let it be Sundance... Please God, I love her..., she can't be dead!

When they arrived within a certain distance, they realized it was Sundance by the color of her coat, and the white spot on the tip of her nose. Luke slowed his pace from the fear of what he was going to encounter, as Bob moved cautiously ahead. Getting down on his knees next to her, he gently laid his head on her chest for a heartbeat. As Luke stood near, he questioned Bob fearing the worse.

"Is she…, is she dead?"

Bob turned with a solemn look, as Luke swallowed the lump in his throat. His heart began to press with anguish waiting for Bob's response.

Finally he answered. "No son, she's not dead; but her breathing is really slow. And seeing how she is down like this, she must be hurt. Horses rarely lay flat on the ground, so I'm thinking she might have fell on the icy roads and possibly has internal injuries. Or perhaps a coyote has bitten her and now she's infected with rabies."

Luke swallowed his emotions. "Is there anything you can do for her Mr. Harper?"

"No son I can't. Only a veterinarian would be able to diagnose what she has for sure. And I'm sorry to say, we don't have one locally in town. The nearest vet is over an hour away in Spokane, and with these snow conditions, it might not be until tomorrow before all the roads are cleared. I'm afraid by the time someone could come out here; it will probably be too late."

Luke knelt on his knees beside her. Ben and his father walked over to see Sundance lying motionless. With tears welling in his eyes, he looked up to his father and saw something totally unexpected…, his father had tears in his eyes also. After looking to his father, Luke turned his attention back to Sundance.

"Oh Sundance, please be alright, I want you to be okay…, you have to be!"

As Luke affectionately patted her neck, suddenly, her ears twitched. She lifted her head off the ground, as Luke wrapped his arms around her neck and hugged her tight.

"Sundance…, oh Sundance!"

Startled to see Luke by her side, she quickly got off the ground. Bob and Luke stood in utter amazement. Then shaking off the snow which had fallen during the night, she held a wide yawn and set her front-leg forward stretching out the sleep from her body. Once again as if to greet him, she nodded her head up and down, as Luke warmly rubbed the bridge of her nose. Then taking a couple of steps to the left, she walked up to Ben and began to smell his chest and arms.

Ben reached out to greet her. "Hi Sundance, I'm so glad you're alright."

Coming to the realization of what was going on, Bob turned to Luke with excitement resonating from his voice.

"Luke…, there was nothing wrong with her; she was just in a deep sleep. Apparently she laid flat on the ground in front of these big boulders to get out of the cold wind - what a smart girl!"

Just then the sun peeked over the top of the hills so that it cast its warm rays upon her. Then to everyone's amazement, she began to walk around in circles while bobbing her head up and down - first to the left, and then to the right. As she did that, she bucked in the air several times and suddenly bolted-off running into the snow covered meadow. Upon seeing this playful behavior, Luke turned to Bob in amazement.

"Mr. Harper…, did she just do what I think she was doing?"

His voice filled with excitement. "Yes! She sure did Luke…, she was dancing!"

"Wow, look at her go Mr. Harper…! Here I thought she might be dead, but instead she's running and playing with more life than I have ever seen before!"

Mr. Dawson walked over and warmly placed his arms around his sons' shoulders.

"You know boys…; I think we have just witnessed a couple of Christmas miracles today. First Ben is going to be alright by what Doctor Friedman told us; and now it looks like Sundance is going to be just fine too."

As they stood there watching Sundance run wild and free in that snow covered meadow, they could tell she ran with contentment and a sense of belonging. Content with the feeling that she served a great purpose in saving Ben…; and with a sense of belonging that she now had someone in Luke who would love and care for her for the rest of her life…

Epilogue

As I recall these events in my mind, I walked to my closet and took down my old Smith Corona typewriter. I thought since that typewriter was a part of this story, I would write the final page on it - it only seemed fitting.

As I sit here thinking of the next lines to write, I see a picture on my desk of Sundance running in the snow. Many years have passed since that fateful Christmas, as my wife Carrie and I are now raising two children of our own. Carrie and I started to officially date in our sophomore year in high school. And although we had been close friends for many years, it wasn't until I gave her a "real kiss," that I knew she was the one for me.

After Bob and his wife retired and moved to Florida to live in a warmer climate…, Carrie and I bought Harper's Feed and Stables. We were thinking of changing the name to "Dawson's Feed & Stables," but Harper's has been a tradition in our town, so we wanted to keep it that way. My mother and father moved to Spokane when the three of us were grown and out of the house. I say the three of us, as Ben did in fact have Addison's disease. With medication, Ben began to get stronger and stronger with each passing day. And it wasn't too long before he stopped reading about sports in magazines, and started to play them for our local high school. Ben is now a healthy man who lives with his wife in Spokane not far from my parents place. He entered the medical field, where he works with people who have disabling illnesses.

After the incident where Ben and Sundance got lost in the snow storm, it wasn't too long before Ben officially gave Sundance to me. So even though I didn't receive the gift I wanted in the beginning, as a result of what happened that day…, I got so much more in the end.

In the spring of that year my father bought Dusty from Mr. Harper, so Ben and I could go riding together. Mr. Harper was fine in selling him the horse, as he said that once Sundance left to live with us, Dusty missed her something awful. Then about a year later we found out just how close Sundance and Dusty really were; as Sundance had a little foal of her own. We called the little foal Sunbeam, as when the sun would cast a beam of sunshine on her nose, she would sneeze like crazy. It was so much fun when Sundance and I would go riding, as little Sunbeam would try to run after us to be by her mother's side. Mattie declared Sunbeam to be hers, and after she was of age, Mattie and I would go riding in those wide open meadows. Mattie is now a grown young woman and is just about ready to graduate from college. She is also involved with youth ministries at our church, and coordinates all of our church plays.

As I think back to that special time in our lives, I think about the sermon that Pastor Whitman gave on the parable of the vineyard. At the time when I agreed to work for Mr. Harper, I understood the money I would make was going to be used to enjoy the Christmas holiday. But like the worker of the vineyard who started at the first hour, I became angry when I felt that my father had treated me unfairly. However, what I didn't know at the time… was that God had a plan. And had it not been for my father giving Sundance to Ben, the miracle of her taking him to Doctor Friedman's would have never happened, and my brother probably would have died that year.

Sundance also got something special that day…, she got her joy back. We can only assume that animals have a sense of understanding and can process those things in their minds. Perhaps feeling helpless or a type of guilt when she could not save her mother's life, she fulfilled a great purpose by taking Ben to someone who could save his. In doing so, she found her joy and once again danced in the morning sun.

As I look back at those times in our lives, one of the things that stands out in my mind, were the words my father spoke to me on that Christmas day. When he told me that, "material things in life are so temporary, but the memories of the smiles on their faces will last you a lifetime." How right he was, as it wasn't too long before my mother's coffee maker broke and she had to buy a new one. Mattie stopped playing with Barbie Dolls, and soon that Dream House was collecting dust in the back of our garage. Ben lost interest in riding horses, and before too long…, all those things were soon forgotten. Originally I thought life had treated me unfairly when I didn't receive the gift I wanted for all the work I had done. But the lesson I learned…, was that God has a plan when he gives his gifts to the people of his choosing. And that sometimes, the gift you don't receive… can be the best one of all.

Our family has enjoyed many wonderful Christmas's together and I am sure there are many more to come. But the memory of the smiles on their faces will last me a lifetime. And the miracle of a horse named Sundance who saved my brother's life… will be the Christmas I'll never forget…

The End

A message to the reader:

I hope you have enjoyed this book and have come away with a feeling of hope to add to the Christmas season. To see other titles I have written; please visit my website at www.dcreyesauthor.com for a list of current and forthcoming titles.

Thank you.

David C. Reyes

www.ingramcontent.com/pod-product-compliance
Lightning Source LLC
Chambersburg PA
CBHW031522040426
42445CB00009B/345